JB JOSSEY-BASS™

A Wiley Brand

Youth Volunteers

How to Recruit, Train, Motivate and Reward Young Volunteers

Scott C. Stevenson, Editor

WILEY

978-1-118-69189-2   ISBN

978-1-118-70375-5   ISBN (online)

Youth Volunteers:

How to Recruit, Train, Motivate and Reward Young Volunteers

Published by

Stevenson, Inc.

P.O. Box 4528 • Sioux City, Iowa • 51104

Phone 712.239.3010 • Fax 712.239.2166

www.stevensoninc.com

Youth Volunteers: How to Recruit, Train, Motivate and Reward Young Volunteers

TABLE OF CONTENTS

Youth Volunteers: How to Recruit, Train, Motivate and Reward Young Volunteers

TABLE OF CONTENTS

Youth Volunteers: How to Recruit, Train, Motivate and Reward Young Volunteers

FIRST STEPS FOR STARTING A YOUTH VOLUNTEER EFFORT

There are many reasons why any volunteer program should include a youth component: young people can become passionate about projects that excite them; they want to prove themselves; they can think outside the box more readily than many adults; and most importantly, they deserve the opportunity to experience the joy of volunteering at a young age. Let's explore some of the essential elements of getting a youth volunteer program up and running.

Tips for Launching a Youth Volunteer Program

When developing a youth volunteer program it makes sense to model it after adult programs. Your program will be successful if it is youth-led and youth-driven from the start.

Here are 12 tips to get your youth program started:

1. Hire at least one teenager part time to help run the program.
2. Set up a leadership/advisory council made up of teens and supportive (and respectful) adults with a youth majority.
3. Put a volunteer management system in place to help recruit, train, place, track and celebrate youth participation.
4. Work with service sites to make projects and staff youth friendly.
5. Recruit and train adult volunteers to support youth service (transportation, reflection, mentoring, co-leading projects, etc.).
6. Create a youth project coordinator leadership slot for youth on each project. Have this person take the lead on organizing the group, communicating with the project site and facilitating the service and reflection.
7. Provide transportation to help make opportunities available to all youth.
8. Develop a structured, verbal reflection activity to be used after every project ("What, So What, Now What?" works well if facilitated with skill).
9. Let teens evaluate each project and act on their suggestions.
10. Make projects meaningful, fun and able to show results.
11. Avoid projects that have teens do meaningless tasks, especially those without interaction with other people.
12. Don't avoid social justice, social action, youth organizing projects — you're developing active, thoughtful citizens here!

Five Keys to Involving Youth as Volunteers

Young people volunteer for many reasons. Those reasons may be to gain job experience, bank community service hours, explore careers, make a difference, build their resumes, learn new skills, have a say in an organization and/or to work with adults as partners.

To attract youth volunteers, your organization should employ five key areas of volunteer management — recruitment, training, supervision, evaluation and recognition — catering to your younger target group. Here's how:

1. **Recruit youths where they are.** Look for volunteers at youth organizations (4-H, Scouts, Boys & Girls Club, etc.), public schools, church youth groups, mentoring programs, teen Web pages, on displays at libraries or schools, and community bulletin boards.
2. **Provide hands-on training.** Relate volunteer work to current skills learned in school, at youth organizations, etc. Relate volunteer work to skills needed for the future. Provide job descriptions and make those jobs meaningful. Pair new volunteers with peer mentors.
3. **Lead more than supervise.** Supervise in a way that doesn't make them feel they are being supervised. Be available/accessible. Treat them with respect. Ask them questions. Plan with youth what they will do.
4. **Allow youth to evaluate themselves.** Allow youth to set their own goals, with your support. When the job is completed, allow them to evaluate whether goals were met. The supervisor can also provide feedback.
5. **Tailor recognition to youths' interests.** Give gift certificates from music or clothing stores and fast food restaurants. Put their names in the community newspaper or agency newsletter. Create thank-you banners. Give photos of them volunteering. Write letters of recommendation.

FIRST STEPS FOR STARTING A YOUTH VOLUNTEER EFFORT

Develop a Skills Profile for Youth Volunteer Positions

A typical volunteer position description explains the purpose and role of the position in the context of the organization, indicates the level of responsibility and outlines the major tasks and responsibilities of the volunteer. However, if your aim is to cultivate learning and skills development, a much more detailed approach is needed.

Start by breaking the position down into its component parts.

Youth Program Leader Skills Profile
- Leadership
- Interpersonal
- Oral communication
- Coaching and mentoring
- Teamwork
- Teaching and training
- Supervising
- Planning
- Organizational
- Creative thinking
- Decision-making
- Problem-solving

Analyze each activity to identify what types of skills and knowledge are central (that is, the minimum level of skills needed to perform the tasks). Then, determine which skills a volunteer could develop through training. By listing these two sets of skills, you can create a skills profile for each position or task.

When considering which skills could be developed in a given assignment, you might want to highlight the skills that could be readily transferred to the job market.

Could Your Nonprofit Benefit From Parental Permission Form?

Many nonprofit organizations successfully utilize the talents of young people as volunteers. If properly supervised and motivated, young people can provide a great service to any group.

Nonprofit officials, however, want to be sure that parents are aware of their minor children's volunteer work. The State of Florida Health Department has a great many young volunteers in several of its programs, and officials require parents of volunteers 18 years old and younger to sign a permission form.

Jeannette Hartzell, director for the division of public and private partnerships for the Palm Beach County Health Department in West Palm Beach, says they use a parental permission form that is part of the state's policies and procedures manual used by all their offices. Out of 376 total volunteers at their seven health centers, they have about 42 junior volunteers between the ages of 14 and 18. Each must have a parent or guardian sign the form.

Young people in the program work during their summer and school breaks and although the amount of time donated by a junior volunteer varies, Hartzell says they recommend shifts not exceed 40 hours a week. "We suggest to the parents that their children don't work eight hours a day, 40 hours a week," says Hartzell. "That's too much for kids on their summer break. And it's difficult to keep the kids from being bored. They tend not to stay focused if they work too long." That recommendation is included

on the permission form signed by the parents.

Although they've never had a parent balk at signing the permission form, Hartzell says if a parent refused, "We'd thank them for their interest but we wouldn't have the child volunteer with us."

Once completed, the form becomes part of the junior volunteer's packet that is kept on file. Even though they've never had an incident where they needed the parental permission form, Hartzell says, "I've been very glad we had these forms. It assures us that the parent knows where the youth is, and we like to talk with the parents to explain our commitment to them and the youth's commitment to us."

Source: Jeanette Hartzell, Director Division of Public/Private Partnerships, State of Florida, Palm Beach County Health Department, West Palm Beach, FL. Phone (561) 355-3013. E-mail: jeanette_freeman@doh.state.fl.us

Content not available in this edition

FIRST STEPS FOR STARTING A YOUTH VOLUNTEER EFFORT

Guidelines Help in Selecting Top Youth

Offer young people rewarding opportunities to give of their time and you may just have a volunteer for life.

Engaging and challenging teens in volunteering opportunities is the goal of the Teen Scene volunteer program at University Hospital Case Medical Center (UHCMC) in Cleveland, OH. Carol Polivchak, manager of volunteer services, says the program utilizes the efforts of 100 teen volunteers each summer (mid-June through mid-August).

The program is not only a benefit to the patients and staff of UHCMC, Polivchak says, it gives teens hands-on experience in a multitude of volunteer roles.

"It's inspiring to see the transformation that takes place during a short period of time," says Polivchak, who begins accepting applications for the highly successful summer program each January. "Many teens begin the program reserved and lacking confidence; by the end of the program, they have gained confidence and are much more articulate."

Because the Teen Scene volunteer program has gained such prominence over its six-year run, the hospital receives far more applications than there are spaces available.

With acceptance to the volunteer program so competitive, the volunteer services manager says, UHCMC has developed a strict series of guidelines to help select the top candidates.

Those guidelines are:

1. The candidate must write answers to essay questions about the position.

2. A guidance counselor must evaluate the student volunteer.

3. During the interview process, students tour their areas of interest to ensure they are up for the challenge of that position. Placing applicants in the environment allows them to confirm whether that is the best placement for them.

4. Remain strict on policies. UHCMC allows only one week off for student volunteers. Those volunteers requiring two weeks off during the program are not accepted.

5. Gain parental commitment to student volunteer schedules and to transporting volunteers who cannot drive themselves.

6. Be firm on deadlines. Accept no applications after the posted registration date.

7. Be compassionate to those who are not accepted and encourage them to apply the following year.

Source: Carol Polivchak, Manager of Volunteer Services, University Hospital Case Medical Center, Cleveland, OH. Phone (216) 844-1504. E-mail: carol.polivchak@uhhospitals.org

Expand Opportunities With Junior Volunteer Program

Engage young volunteers and you just may have a volunteer for life.

Through its junior volunteer program, Antelope Valley Hospital (Lancaster, CA) has more than 200 volunteers age 14 to 18 who assist with reception, the gift shop, patient care and more.

Geri Nunez, volunteer coordinator, started the junior volunteer program three years ago. She shares suggestions to create a successful program:

1. **Have an open mind and give young people a chance.** She suggests working with youth who have a grade point average of 2.0 or greater to allow for children from a variety of backgrounds to participate and succeed.

2. **Conduct a thorough orientation outlining expectations for the participants and their parents.** Nunez, for instance, tells students they're expected to make the call, not their parents, if they're sick or late. She also clearly defines that the students are to treat their volunteer role as a job.

3. **Allow the junior volunteers to lead.** At the hospital, junior volunteers organize a variety of fundraisers for the hospital, including an annual bake sale. Nunez allows the volunteers to organize and manage these events, offering guidance as needed. Funds from these events — averaging $3,000 a year — are used to purchase needed equipment for the hospital.

4. **Conduct regular junior volunteer meetings** to offer guidance, share ideas and create a sense of routine for the program.

5. **Create a board for the junior volunteer program.** Organize an election for offices of president, vice president, secretary and treasurer. Teens who volunteered 100 hours or more at the hospital campaign for these offices.

Nunez has developed a strong rapport with her student volunteers and has found that by being approachable and open minded, she has been able to develop a group of exceptional volunteers.

Source: Geri Nunez, Volunteer Coordinator, Antelope Valley Hospital, Lancaster, CA. Phone (661) 949-5109. E-mail: geri.nunez@AVHospital.org

Nurture Junior Volunteers, Create Volunteers for Life

Even the youngest volunteer can make a difference, says Sherry Hodnett, volunteer and bereavement coordinator, Home Hospice of West Texas (Big Spring, TX), who started the Hospice Halos youth volunteer program three years ago.

Hospice Halos are volunteers age 11 to 14 who assist Hodnett once a week in serving hospice clients. They serve food, read to residents, call bingo, give manicures, help with events and bring roses to families of patients who have died.

Hodnett recommends these steps to create your junior volunteer program:

1. **Spread the word** to volunteers that you're starting a new program and would like to involve their children, grandchildren, nieces and nephews.

2. **Host an orientation meeting** to discuss expectations with volunteers and parents. Share a list of expected tasks so there are no surprises. Have volunteer and parent sign a letter stating they are expected to volunteer one day a week, plus waivers or confidentiality forms. Be specific on policies for cell phones, iPods, etc. Inform parents how to reach children during volunteer shifts.

3. **Provide complete training and/or in-services needed to begin volunteering.** This includes any tests or screenings, such as tuberculosis tests.

4. **Begin activities under supervision.** Provide and require volunteers to wear T-shirts or badges that identify them as volunteers.

5. **Add youth volunteers to your mailing lists** so they and their parents receive the latest newsletters or correspondence to stay informed on upcoming events and activities.

6. **At the end of the program or at your annual recognition event, reward youth volunteers** with positive feedback, certificates or a field trip to thank them for their participation. Have the volunteers complete a letter of interest to participate in the program in the upcoming year.

Source: Sherry Hodnett, Volunteer and Bereavement Coordinator, Home Hospice of West Texas, Big Spring, TX.
Phone (432) 264-7599. E-mail: bshodnett@hotmail.com

Consider Asking for Letters of Recommendation

Asking teen volunteers and interns for letters of recommendation is one way to make sure they will be committed to the role. Since commitment is so important in volunteering, why not ask all volunteers for letters of recommendation?

Amanda Vallozzi, manager of volunteer services, The George Washington University Hospital (Washington, DC), requires new volunteers to turn in three letters of recommendation before they can attend orientation.

With an average of 60 new applications every other month, Vallozzi says being able to determine which applicants will take the role seriously and stick with the commitment is crucial. She says she has had volunteers drop out after just a few weeks, and requiring letters of recommendation helps narrow down the field to persons who definitely want to stick around.

"We don't want to waste our time and resources and we don't want to waste the volunteer's time if they're not serious about the position," she says.

Letters can be written by anyone the volunteer has known for at least a year, except for immediate family. Letters typically come from employers, teachers, professors, friends and neighbors. Vallozzi tells volunteers the letters should read as if the volunteer is applying for a job, detailing personality, strengths and commitment. Letters must be typed (handwritten letters may be accepted if a phone number is included), and Vallozzi says they usually contact at least one of the writers for more information about the applicant.

Requiring letters of recommendation hasn't been a deterrent to recruiting volunteers, she emphasizes. In fact, Vallozzi says volunteers who are serious about the position (which is what Vallozzi hoped to learn by requiring the letters) are happy to provide them.

She notes that the hospital is known for high-caliber volunteers who are punctual, adhere to a strict dress code and are serious about their roles.

Source: Amanda Vallozzi, Manager, Volunteer Services, The George Washington University Hospital, Washington, DC.
Phone (202) 715-4188.
E-mail: Amanda.vallozzi@gwu-hospital.com

Youth Volunteers: How to Recruit, Train, Motivate and Reward Young Volunteers

TIPS & TECHNIQUES FOR RECRUITING YOUTH

The places where you may look for young volunteers, and the ways in which you recruit them, may differ from adult volunteers. Even the ways in which you capture a young person's attention will vary. You may find, for instance, that it's easier to get a young person involved in one activity for a brief period of time and then ease him/her into longer-term projects. Likewise, what you offer as volunteer opportunities will impact young peoples' willingness to join in with a project.

How to Find Quality Junior Volunteers

How do you determine which applicants make quality junior volunteers?

Mary Rahaim, director of volunteer services, The William W. Backus Hospital (Norwich, CT), says for her organization it's important to find youth still in high school who are willing to learn, be accepting of others, understand the importance of privacy and have a professional attitude.

Rahaim has developed a system to find the most qualified candidates. The following is her process:

1. **Send information packets to local high schools.** Rahaim sends about 30 information packets to local high schools in eastern Connecticut. The packets include program information, applications and Rahaim's business card.

2. **Conduct personal interviews.** Rahaim interviews each applicant with a parent or guardian present. "It's important for the families to know what the expectations are so we're all on the same page regarding orientation, attendance and being professional," says Rahaim. During the interview, she observes the candidate's eye contact, alertness, interest in what she is saying and if the applicant asks questions.

3. **Contact references.** "On the application, I ask for a school reference who is mailed an applicant evaluation form. The form rates the youth's ability to accept direction, express feelings and work independently and on creativity, dependability and maturity," says Rahaim. "I also ask them to list three adjectives that best describe the applicant. These words are a tell-tale sign of what the applicant is like."

Rahaim says the junior volunteer program is limited to 100 volunteers, which include successful junior volunteers from the previous summer. Once the students are accepted, they must attend an eight-hour classroom orientation including fire safety, policy and procedure, hospital tour and a bed-making and stretcher/wheel chair training.

Source: Mary Rahaim, Director of Volunteer Services, The William W. Backus Hospital, Norwich, CT. Phone (860) 823-6320. E-mail: mrahaim@wwbh.org

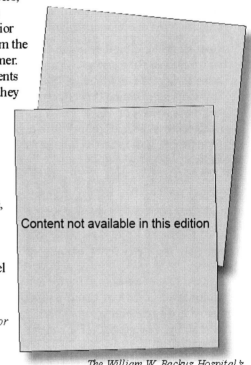

Content not available in this edition

The William W. Backus Hospital's junior volunteer application form and school reference form.

Simple Strategies Work Wonders at Volunteer Fair

When taking part in events that feature many booths for visitors to peruse, take a page from organizers of Volunteer Day at a Midwest mall. Wanting optimal exposure, recruiting opportunities and program promotion for every agency, organizers devised a few tricks:

✓ **To encourage participation,** shoppers received bingo-type cards with 15 squares. They received a stamp in a square at each booth they visited, encouraging interaction with the volunteers. Filled cards went in a drawing for a grand prize.

✓ **To attract people to a display,** agencies were encouraged to offer freebies such as candy, gum, pens, balloons, hats, coloring books and first-aid kits. These small gimmicks gave volunteers plentiful opportunity to interact with guests and answer their questions and distribute program information.

✓ **To draw people to a presentation,** offering refreshments, pins and an opportunity for a photo with the celebrity speaker worked like magic.

TIPS & TECHNIQUES FOR RECRUITING YOUTH

Volunteer Recruiting Dos and Don'ts

There are some simple guidelines to follow to make your next recruiting effort a successful one. Follow these tips when recruiting new volunteers:

- ❏ Do work to recruit new volunteers by getting them involved in a one-time activity.
- ❏ Don't ask just anyone to volunteer. Do set a goal and determine which individuals from your community will best deliver for your nonprofit.
- ❏ Do be up-front about time commitment necessary to volunteer at your organization.
- ❏ Don't recruit using guilt methods or by acting desperate.
- ❏ Do allow a potential volunteer to say no gracefully.
- ❏ Don't oversimplify what will be required of volunteers. Hand them a detailed volunteer job description whenever possible.

- ❏ Do be enthusiastic and upbeat when talking to current and potential volunteers (and everyone else) about your organization.
- ❏ Don't downplay the importance of volunteers. Explain to new recruits how valued volunteers are and how your organization will recognize their efforts.
- ❏ Do allow volunteers the opportunity to ease into volunteering by first starting with a one-time or episodic volunteering effort or to begin with limited hours.
- ❏ Don't sugarcoat the volunteer's role, but at the same time, don't overemphasize the negative aspects of the role, either. Try to paint a realistic picture.
- ❏ Do give specific examples of long-term volunteers who have successfully assisted in your organization and make such persons available to new volunteers as mentors and sources of information and support.

Revved-up Brochure Boosts Youth Volunteers

Sarah Lewan, coordinator of volunteer resources at the American Red Cross of Greater Columbus (OH), used her background in working with young people to pump up her youth volunteer program.

Lewan worked with the Red Cross marketing department to create brochures and posters targeting youth volunteers. Then she contacted 43 area high schools for permission to send each 20 brochures and two posters. Everyone said yes. If a school had a service club, she targeted the service club directly through her cover letter. Otherwise, the packets went to the guidance offices.

The idea for youth recruitment brochures and posters came out of necessity as Lewan and staff sought to grow their little-known youth program, she says. They were creating youth volunteer positions with responsibilities similar to those for adults. "We didn't want a club," she says. "We wanted youth volunteer positions that really benefited the organization."

Through a partnership with AmeriCorps, the American Red Cross of Greater Columbus received grant money specifically for print items.

Lewan says the efforts are paying off. By getting materials to schools right after spring break, she received more calls for summer youth volunteer opportunities.

Source: Sarah Lewan, Coordinator, Volunteer Resources, American Red Cross of Greater Columbus, Columbus, OH. Phone (614) 253-2740. E-mail: lewans@usa.redcross.org

Tips for Successful Youth Recruitment

If you want your printed materials to appeal to youth, keep these tips in mind, says Sarah Lewan, coordinator of volunteer resources for the American Red Cross of Greater Columbus (OH), who recently revamped a brochure for youth volunteers:

- ✓ **Think eye-catching and unusual.** If your budget allows, go for different-shaped materials. Have fun. Lewan's first wish for a cross-shaped brochure was beyond her budget. So instead she put lettering all around the outside of the open brochure. Readers had to rotate it as they read it, making for a more interesting brochure.

- ✓ **Use pictures of youth to really make a connection.** Lewan used pictures of her youth volunteers in the brochure and on posters.

- ✓ **Tap college, high school print shops.** They can save you money and may donate their efforts. Lewan got a college print shop to do two-sided, full-color posters for 30 cents each.

- ✓ **Get creative with two colors.** Printing with more colors costs more. But color attracts attention. Lewan used black and red inks to make the brochure stand out yet keep overall costs low.

Content not available in this edition

TIPS & TECHNIQUES FOR RECRUITING YOUTH

Use the Media to Recruit Young Volunteers

Access to a steady supply of new and enthusiastic volunteers is a goal of nearly every charitable organization. And getting the message out to young, would-be volunteers takes some special doing. That's where the media can help in recruitment efforts.

Most news media are interested in stories about youth who are doing worthwhile volunteer projects. You may be able to develop some successful strategies to attract youngsters to your roster by offering programs and volunteer opportunities that have a dual objective: adding to your base of support both now and in the future, and training youth who will become future leaders themselves. To do so:

- **Identify assignments in your organization that young volunteers can complete.** Once you have found a variety of jobs for the entry-level volunteer, schedule them for weekends and after school hours when students' hours are more flexible. Send news releases to news media outlining the work schedules. Make it known that youth are the focus of your recruitment efforts. When enough youth have agreed to participate, schedule a festive kickoff meeting with food, T-shirts, music and an organizational rally. Invite photographers and reporters to attend. Have press packages for them to use for reference material in future coverage.

- **Explore the concept of youth internships in your organization.** Many youth search for positive work and civic involvement experiences to use on resumes or for scholarship and college entrance applications. Your organization can help provide these. Interview school guidance counselors, churches or other organization who share in your philosophies to determine which kinds of opportunities are most useful to students.

When solid objectives are defined, prepare formal media announcements detailing your plans, and inviting community youth to participate.

- **Ask parents to involve their teenaged children or their friends.** Like the popular take-your-daughter/son-to-work-day observed by many businesses, borrow a similar approach with a bring-a-youth-to-help project where the first student you ask in turn brings another, until each has asked or recruited 10 helpers. The hook of the chain of youth volunteers may be unique enough in your community to attract reporters. Present each participant with certificates of achievement. After the event is over, continue to contact first-time participants to join in other projects.

- **Be selective about the type of youth you select to participate.** Like adults, youth like to feel important, capable and respected. Develop some high-level youth leadership programs designed to attract the cream of the crop in your community, and even offer a scholarship if appropriate. Ask senior volunteers and board members to serve on a selection committee. When criteria are established, hold a press conference about your prestigious new youth program, having your board chairman or best-known volunteer leader preside. Even if all the youth who are interested in being included don't meet the most stringent criteria, offer them other special projects in your organization and opportunities to be future honorees.

Take a look at the ways in which you are recruiting young volunteers today and examine how the media might complement those strategies.

Youth Volunteer Corps Help Get Youth Involved

Do you want to include more young people — say, ages 13 to 17 — in your volunteer program? Connecting with Youth Volunteer Corps of America (YVCA) is a great place to start.

For 20 years, YVCA (Shawnee Mission, KS), has partnered with nonprofits to recruit youth volunteers. YVCA has more than 40 chapters across the United States and Canada.

David Battey, YVCA president and founder, says each chapter works with a sponsoring organization such as a local YMCA, school district, volunteer center, retired senior volunteer program or municipality. Sponsoring organizations provide volunteering opportunities and set up opportunities with other local nonprofits.

Local YVCA program directors contact and meet with nonprofits to find a project for the volunteers. Battey says there are 12 flexible program standards. The project must

allow the volunteers to work as a team and have a start and stop time.

Recent YVCA projects include rebuilding trails, painting murals, feeding the homeless and creating Web pages.

YVCA officials also work with nonprofit groups to come up with creative opportunities for volunteers. For example, YVCA helped a nonprofit group start a four-week summer camp for children. The team leader helped formulate the idea, recruited volunteers and provided the supervision.

Each local YVCA chapter can be contacted directly from the website. The website, www.yvca.org also has information on how to start a chapter and receive funding assistance from the national office.

Source: David Battey, President and Founder, Youth Volunteer Corps of America, Shawnee Mission, KS. Phone (913) 432-9822. E-mail: dbattey@yvca.org

Unique Brochure Captures Teens' Attention

When seeking teen volunteers, you need a recruitment tool that grabs their attention and relates to their lives.

The teen volunteer brochure for Hospice of the Valley (Phoenix, AZ), does both.

Kathy Miller, teen program manager, says staff wanted to show teens the similarities they have with hospice patients — many of whom are senior citizens. So they created a brochure that folds out to a large poster. Each fold tells a story as it reveals a picture of an older adult with a statement relating to his/her earlier life: "I am a cheerleader," "I am a linebacker," "I am a tutor," I am a prom queen," "I am a drummer," "I am a romeo" and "I am a ballerina."

Miller says the captions connect teens to the fact hospice patients were once teens themselves with the same likes and goals. The poster can be displayed as an eye-catching draw, while the brochures contain information needed for teens to sign on as hospice volunteers.

A local design company helped create the brochures. Hospice staff got friends and family to be the models.

The brochures can be used year round, with timely information, such as training dates, sent as a separate attachment.

Miller says teens have reacted positively to the brochure and the entertaining photos, which, she says, achieves their goal of grabbing teens' attention while also communicating with them on their level about the nature of hospice and what it means to be a teen volunteer.

Content not available in this edition

Content not available in this edition

These photos are from a brochure/poster Hospice of the Valley (Phoenix, AZ) staff use to create common ground between teen volunteers and elderly clients.

Source: Kathy Miller, Teen Program Manager, Hospice of the Valley, Phoenix, AZ. Phone (602) 636-6342. E-mail: kmiller@hov.org

Internet Draws Youth Into Community Service

The most effective way to recruit volunteers from Generation Y (anyone born after 1979) may be through your website.

A new study from American University's Center for Social Media (Washington, D.C.) examines hundreds of websites created to encourage and facilitate youth involvement in civic activities. The study shows that young people use the Internet to participate in and/or educate themselves on a wide range of issues including voting, volunteerism, racism and tolerance, social activism, and, most recently, patriotism, terrorism and military conflict.

According to the study, the Internet's power to expand youth volunteering is most visible in the work of websites such as SERVEnet (www.servenet.org), Idealist (www.idealist.org) and NetAid (www.netaid.org).

What are you doing to tap into this generation of volunteers? Use your website to list youth volunteer opportunities, offer a virtual volunteering section (volunteer activities carried out via the Internet), or create a volunteer resource section pertaining to youth service. If you don't have a website, enlist the help of a young person. Many of today's students are technologically savvy and would be pleased to create an Internet presence for your organization.

See the report summary at: www.centerforsocialmedia.org/ecitizens/index.htm.

For more info:, Barb Gottlieb, AU Center for Social Media. Phone (202) 885-2082. E-mail: gottlieb@american.edu; Maralee Csellar, AU Media Relations. Phone (202) 885-5952. E-mail: csellar@american.edu

Three Ways to Recruit Volunteers Online

Have you ever considered using the Web to recruit volunteers? Following are ways to utilize the Internet to increase your volunteer numbers.

1. **Use an online opportunities list.** Do you include a detailed position description? The more information you can give the better. Attention spans are short; give the surfer as much information as possible, right from the beginning. Also include your e-mail address or create a separate e-mail address just for online recruitment so your current inbox doesn't get overloaded. Most volunteer opportunity lists are free, so put opportunities on multiple sites.

2. **Make sure your website is recruitment friendly.** Put a visible link, like a highlighted box, to your volunteer page on every page of your website, home, other departments, etc. Beyond that have the link list available, volunteer opportunities and an online application. Make signing up to volunteer online as easy as possible.

3. **Create a newsgroup.** A newsgroup is like an online community where its members can chat, receive notices, etc. You can create your own site for your volunteers and direct prospective volunteers to it. Check out groups.google.com for an online tour and instructions to set up your own group.

Attracting Youth Volunteers? Use a Splash of Color!

When staff with the City of Columbia (Columbia, MO) want to catch the attention of teenage volunteers for the city's Youth in Action program, they just drop them a card.

Not just any card — this card, designed specifically for the program, draws teens in with an eye-popping purple and yellow design. Another reason the card stands out is its unusual 6 X 11-inch size.

To create the marketing plan for the program geared to teens ages 12 to 15 years, city staff called on Stephens College design student EmilyAnn Allen.

Leigh Britt, volunteer coordinator, City of Columbia, says they wanted a student who could volunteer time to create a piece they could use for years to come, give the program its own identity and make a statement.

"Local youth are a great audience who can be a great pool of volunteers," Britt says. "They can do just about anything an adult can do, with assistance and guidance."

Britt answers questions about this marketing piece:

"Why did Youth in Action choose to produce this particular piece?"

"Youth volunteers are the key to the Youth in Action program. Volunteers bank more than 300 hours per year to volunteer organizations; we need to reach these volunteers to sustain and grow this program. The postcard will assist in doing that for the next two years."

"What key components does this piece have to catch attention?"

"It's full color and appeals to a teenage group. It was created to appeal to both boys and girls because the color and design are not gender specific. The verbiage used on the postcard emphasizes the fun of volunteering, drawing in the teen reader."

Content not available in this edition

"Is this a cost-effective approach to marketing volunteer opportunities?"

"The postcards were printed by Modern Postcard, which does cost-effective full-color printing. The cost was less than $400 for 1,000 cards that will be used for a few years. Because of the size, the postage was a bit more, but it makes a great impression and gets attention at events and on bulletin boards."

"Why did you use a local college student to create the design?"

"The great thing about working with the college is that you have this fantastic talent and, again, they're volunteering. It's part of their educational experience and it was a good way for us to tap in and get a professional looking piece that otherwise would have cost us hundreds of dollars."

"Are there uses for this piece other than mailing them?"

"The postcard has a dual purpose as it is used at events as handouts to entice youth volunteers and as a mailer."

Source: Leigh Britt, Volunteer Coordinator, City of Columbia, Columbia, MO. Phone (573) 874-7504.
E-mail: lcnutter@GoColumbiaMO.com

TIPS & TECHNIQUES FOR RECRUITING YOUTH

National Program Uses Music to Inspire Youth Into Life-long Volunteering

Boost Mobile Rock Corps (BMRC) of New York, NY, is a national program launched in 2005 with the intention of using music to motivate youth 14 and over to get involved in volunteering. It works by youth giving four hours of volunteer time to earn a big-name concert ticket. Over the past two years BMRC has engaged 16,000 volunteers in 175 community projects.

BMRC recruits, registers and provide music, t-shirts and food for volunteers that take part in approved local nonprofit projects. Lisa Lepson, director of nonprofit services, says the goal is to create life-long volunteers.

Here's how it works:

- BMRC partners with nonprofits throughout Los Angeles, Oakland, Miami, Atlanta, Portland, Houston, Philadelphia, Chicago, New York City, New Orleans and Baltimore to form Non-Profit Partner (NPP). Lepson says a nonprofit must be registered as a 501(c) 3 status, have a three- to five-year operating history, one to two community references from leading civic organizations and ongoing volunteer opportunities for returning RockCorps volunteers.

- NPPs submit a project proposal that addresses a project's need with tangible results. The projects must be completed in four hours by 50 to 200 volunteers, and be designed to accommodate BMRC volunteers. Lepson says projects have included indoor and outdoor beautification projects and helping food banks and soup kitchens.

- BMRC supports the volunteers and the nonprofit by offering a supply budget of $5 per volunteer and works with the NPP to bring additional assets to the project. A point person is assigned to each project and, with their team, provides onsite volunteer supervision. BMRC gives each NPP a letter of agreement outlining how the partnership works and what each organization brings to the table.

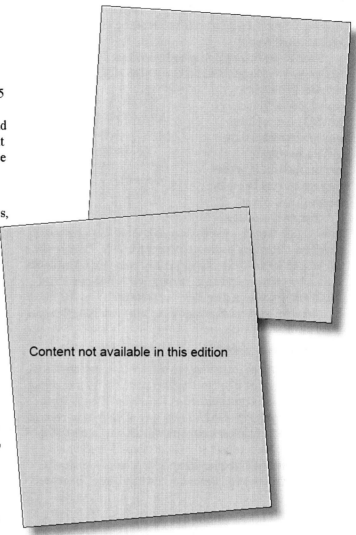

Content not available in this edition

Source: Lisa Lepson, Director of Nonprofit Services, Boost Mobile RockCorps, New York, NY. Phone (212) 938-1172 ext 205. E-mail: llepson@rockcorps.com

Tap Eagle Scout Candidates for Special Projects

Don't overlook Boy Scouts of America as a source of volunteer assistance.

Boy Scouts seeking to achieve the rank of Eagle Scout — an honor reached by just 2 percent of Boy Scouts — are expected to plan a philanthropic project for their communities that generates both volunteers and funds.

Podcasts Reach More Volunteers, Supporters

Podcasts are growing in popularity as means to promote nonprofit efforts, communicate volunteer opportunities and recruit volunteers.

One of the first volunteer centers to host a podcast, Volunteer San Diego (VSD) of San Diego, CA, has become a leader in utilizing social media. Volunteers at VSD have initiated and implemented these efforts, helping to expose thousands of new persons and entities to the nonprofit's services.

A podcast is a pre-recorded audio program posted to a website and made available for download so people can listen to it on personal computers or mobile devices such as mp3 players.

For its first podcast alone, VSD started out with about 100 downloads per month, says Brent Shintani, podcast producer for VSD. "We've since raised it to 30 to 70 downloads per day with more downloads right after each new posting. To date, we've had more than 20,000 downloads in total from our website."

Shintani answers questions about how podcasting benefits VSD's volunteer initiatives.

What is the purpose of the podcasts offered by VSD?

"Initially it was an experiment to reach a new, untapped audience and after that it became another platform for messaging to a different kind of audience — folks who listen to iPods and mp3 players. (It also is) a new way of delivering content to volunteers, volunteer managers and anyone interested in what we do. We received an early response from a volunteer center interested in service-learning in Maine — podcasts allow us to reach an audience beyond San Diego, even overseas!"

Who are podcasts meant for?

"Anyone interested in volunteering or needing volunteers. The great thing about podcasts is that you can tailor them to a specific audience, but you are online so anyone can become your audience."

Is there a cost to hear them?

"There is no cost to download."

How are the podcasts helpful to your organization and its constituents?

"Podcasts make volunteering accessible. They add a voice to volunteers and those involved to get others excited and en-

Tips to Make the Most of Podcasts

Having had significant success in using podcasts to promote volunteer initiatives at Volunteer San Diego (San Diego, CA), Brent Shintani, podcast producer, shares tips for creating and using attention-grabbing podcasts to the fullest:

- **Have a focused vision for the show.** Create a consistent theme for each podcast and always engage viewers with the mission of organization.

- If looking at production value, it's always best to **have different points of view on a variety of different topics** — get the experts in! Go to the folks who know the most and are the most passionate about what you're talking about in your podcast. Create a relaxed atmosphere and just talk. VSD has had great success using an interview format.

- **Try to keep to a consistent schedule to maintain your audience.**

- **Keep topics broad, but offer a timely message.** Podcasts allow you to cover similar topics while adding relevancy with specifics from organizational messaging for a certain time period (e.g., holiday volunteer opportunities or President Obama's call to service).

- **Deliver in any and all mediums.** Don't limit your organization to iTunes or specific feeds. Post everywhere — your organization's website, blog, Facebook, etc. By cross-posting, you can reach a wider audience.

gaged. For some, hearing about other's experiences inspires them to get involved. For volunteer managers and nonprofits, we discuss best practices and anecdotal program support. It provides an informal legitimacy to our information and a community for those interested in service."

Sources: Brent Shintani, Vice President of the Board and Podcast Producer; Kelli Ochoa, Development Director; Volunteer San Diego, San Diego, CA. Phone (858) 636-4133. E-mail: kochoa@volunteersandiego.org

Youth Volunteers: How to Recruit, Train, Motivate and Reward Young Volunteers

HOW TO CONNECT WITH AND MOTIVATE YOUNG PEOPLE

It's one thing to get young people excited about a volunteer project; it's another to keep them energized for longer periods of time. To keep youth motivated, be mindful of their world and learn to connect with them in ways with which they are most comfortable: — social networking sites, text and instant messaging. Seek their input in identifying volunteer opportunities and even incentives that will keep them coming back for more.

Advice to Keep Youth Volunteers Motivated

High school and college-age students are invaluable to the volunteer workforce at Deaconess Medical Center and Valley Hospital and Medical Center (Spokane, WA).

Each student session, employees welcome a new group of student volunteers to help with healthcare tasks and shadow them on the job. Students are allowed access to emergency rooms and, in a highly supervised way, operating viewing rooms.

Joey Frost, director of volunteer services, offers advice regarding specific elements when working with volunteers ages 14 to 22:

❑ **Applicant interview and evaluation** — When you interview youth volunteers, discuss specifics about their commitment level and schedules to determine if they are already too overcommitted with activities and school to make time for volunteer efforts. Frost notes that some applicants apply only to appease wishes of parents or a college application board.

❑ **References** — Just as with any other position, have students apply for volunteer roles. Call on references to learn the student's level of maturity and responsibility before assigning a specific position. At the medical center where Frost supervises volunteers, staff help determine applicants' ability to handle emergency situations.

❑ **Flexibility** — Student volunteers need flexibility in their schedules to accommodate course work. By creating a flexible scheduling plan, Deaconess and Valley garnered a more dedicated volunteer base. During quiet times, information and guest relations desk volunteers are allowed to study while on duty, giving them necessary study time while fulfilling a useful role.

❑ **Variety** — Responsibility and variety help young people stay excited about volunteering. Frost allows students to move into various areas of the healthcare system each semester to give them a varied exposure and keep them engaged.

❑ **Boundaries** — Be clear as to the rules of your organization. With cell phone and iPod usage skyrocketing among teens, Frost makes it clear that these devices are not allowed during volunteer shifts.

❑ **Policy review** — Provide volunteers and their parents with a copy of the procedure manual for your institution. Have both the volunteer and parents sign a form stating they've carefully read the manual to prevent future misunderstandings.

❑ **Program evaluation** — Utilize your current youth volunteers to determine areas of improvement needed in your program. After speaking with high school volunteers who expressed boredom with some volunteer roles, Frost found she could combine two service areas — pharmacy delivery and front desk — to keep volunteers busy and more efficient in their volunteer efforts.

Source: Joey Frost, Director of Volunteer Services, Deaconess Medical Center and Valley Hospital and Medical Center, Spokane, WA. Phone (509) 473-3767. E-mail: FrostJ@Empirehealth.org

Let's Get Youth Excited About Volunteering

Whether it's your own son or daughter, other relative or the child of a friend or associate, think about what you might do to interest a young person in volunteering.

There is no time like youth to begin conveying the virtues of volunteering. If you can expose youth to this noble endeavor early on, you can open them up to its rewards and help them to establish positive volunteering habits.

It's been said, "The more you lose yourself in caring about others, the more trivial your own worries and problems become."

Teaching young people to become involved as volunteers and to care about others helps reduce their life's stresses and moves the focus from them to others.

Do your part to involve youth in volunteering. Use any of these examples to get started:

✓ Tell your children or others about your volunteer involvement. Let them know the ways in which you assist other organizations.

✓ If and when it's possible, bring the young adults with you to meetings or assist you with volunteer tasks to get a flavor of the experience.

✓ Help the young person research and find a volunteer opportunity that could be rewarding for him/her. If the individual is college bound, explain that past leadership experiences are taken into consideration for both admissions and scholarship awards.

HOW TO CONNECT WITH AND MOTIVATE YOUNG PEOPLE

Communicate With Teens in Language They Understand

For persons who do not fall into the age range of 13 to 19, teenagers may seem like they come from a different planet. Communicating with teens as a volunteer manager can be daunting as you wonder if your message is having an impact.

To help guarantee your important information gets to your young volunteers, speak in their language. Use one or all of these teen-friendly techniques to get your message across:

✓ **Text messaging.** Send mass text messaging updates about your volunteer program to all volunteers with cell phones. Text-savvy teens will appreciate your efforts to communicate at their preferred level. Check with your cell phone provider to ensure you have an unlimited texting plan to prevent additional costs.

✓ **Facebook.** Set up a Facebook page at www.facebook.com specifically for your teen volunteers. Use this free online social network to post volunteer-relevant topics, schedules and events. Volunteers who sign up as fans of the page will receive automatic notification when content is updated.

✓ **Internet presence.** Create a Web page specifically geared to teen volunteers. Add a page to your current website that makes announcements and includes updates for your teen volunteers, along with volunteer activities, group schedules and kudos for teens who deserve a pat on the back.

Teen Volunteers: From 'Do I Have to?' to 'Love to!'

For many teens, the motivation for volunteering comes from parental pressure or the need to fulfill a requirement. Many volunteer managers admit teens come to volunteer with the attitude: "Do I have to?"

But teens can also become engaged in your cause and want to come on their own.

Tish Sammon, community resources coordinator, city of Monterey (Monterey, CA), says her VolunTeen program targets teens from the perspective of workforce readiness. Teens want to be involved because they can gain valuable work skills in a fun environment.

The program, for teens aged 13 to 16 (before they can legally work and have other opportunities), teaches workplace skills, plus provides teens with resources and references for future employment.

Sammon says the program's goals are to generate a culture of service in teens and help them feel valued.

For the teens, all phases of the volunteering program parallel the working world, she says. They are interviewed for the position and are required to fill out a time sheet. Staff act as workforce mentors to the teens. The teens work under staff supervision.

Sammon says the idea is to allow teens to gain valuable skills, which could lead to a future job within the city.

The teens volunteer 10 hours a week. Many of the opportunities lie in the recreation department, where teens can choose to volunteer with the sports camps, cheerleading camp, pools, library, harbor department, maintenance staff, video/website development or administration. Each teen is placed in the opportunity based on his/her interests.

Sammon says the program is a huge draw. Many teens are excited to come because they not only feel valued, they gain skills and connections for their future. The program is also a good recruiting tool, she says, noting that some opportunities, like the sports and cheerleading camps, give teens the opportunity to work with younger people who get excited about joining the program themselves.

Source: Tish Sammon, Community Resources Coordinator, City of Monterey, Monterey, CA. Phone (831) 646-3719. E-mail: sammon@ci.monterey.ca.us

Consider Instant Messaging for Young Volunteers

The medium you choose for communicating information to your volunteers may vary from one group to another. For example, younger volunteers tend to want their information in quick-hit fashion typical of the digital age, whereas older volunteers who grew up reading newspapers will appreciate a more complete type of media, such as a newsletter. For the younger generation, try some sort of instant-messaging system. Volunteers in their 20s are the first generation to grow up on these systems that send quick messages in real time, in a format similar to conversation.

HOW TO CONNECT WITH AND MOTIVATE YOUNG PEOPLE

Consider Out-of-the-ordinary Field Trips for Volunteers

Remember school field trips? You were so excited you couldn't sleep the night before! Something new. Something fun. A day away from the normal routine — with friends!

Field trips don't have to be just for students. They can be a great way to encourage friendship and fellowship in your volunteers while also providing a fun and possibly educational adventure. Here are six reasons to invest time in field trips:

1. **A way to say thanks.** Field trips offer an additional way to reward volunteers for their gift of time to your organization and those you serve.

2. **A means to attract new volunteers.** Being able to tell would-be volunteers about some of your recent field trips could help with recruitment efforts.

3. **An opportunity to learn.** Some field trips may serve as educational opportunities for volunteers that may, in fact, benefit your organization in return.

4. **A chance to sing your praises.** Your volunteers will spread good news about your organization as they tell friends, families and acquaintances of their adventure.

5. **A tactic to inspire volunteers.** Off-site adventures will energize your volunteers and reinforce their loyalty to your organization.

6. **A way to combat volunteer burn-out.** Volunteers will enjoy a day away from their busy day-to-day routines. A small field trip will be just the relaxation they need to rejuvenate themselves

Consider offering quarterly or even monthly field trips for some or all of your volunteers. Explore field trip possibilities that may provide beyond-the-norm experiences. For example, if your organization has a major corporate partner, consider a visit to that corporate location where your volunteers can enjoy a tour and meet with a select group of the corporation's employees. See additional trip ideas, below.

Field Trip Ideas to Recharge, Reward, Inspire Volunteers

Here are volunteer fields trip ideas to get you started:

✓ Tour another agency with a connection to your mission or services.

✓ Arrange a trip to one of your satellite locations. Have persons who benefit from or witness benefits of your organization share their stories.

✓ Secure donated tickets to a sporting event, complete with a tailgate party. Have your group recognized on the loudspeaker or scoreboard.

✓ Exchange field trip hosting duties with another nonprofit organization.

✓ Take a bus to meet with your chapters throughout the state or region. Come prepared to share volunteer success stories, and have them do the same.

✓ Tour a business or other entity with a connection to your organization (i.e., take library volunteers to a book bindery or printer; church volunteers to a bible camp; humane society volunteers to the zoo).

✓ Relive field trip memories of school days in just-for-fun outings to museums, cultural sites or theatres.

✓ Indulge volunteers with a brunch trip to a bed-and-breakfast, day trip to an arts/crafts or renaissance fair.

Encourage Your Volunteers to Form an Online Chat Group

Looking to connect your volunteers and possibly attract younger persons to your volunteer ranks? Consider establishing an online chat group.

Online chat groups are free and easy to set up. Many of the main search engines, like Yahoo.com, offer this service.

Kathy Cahill, volunteer services coordinator, Lee County Parks and Recreation (Fort Myers, FL), says one of her groups of volunteers established and maintains an online chat group specifically for its location. The group is a great way for the volunteers to recruit within each other and stay connected, she says.

While the group is completely volunteer-run, Cahill did set some guidelines with the volunteers to make sure the content was appropriate. All content must be related to volunteers and/or wetland conservation.

Source: Kathy Cahill, Volunteer Services Coordinator, Lee County Parks and Recreation, Fort Myers, FL. Phone (239) 432-2159. E-mail: kcahill@leegov.com

HOW TO CONNECT WITH AND MOTIVATE YOUNG PEOPLE

Teen Incentive Program Increases Hours

Amy Krueger, junior volunteer assistant at St. Cloud Hospital (St. Cloud, MN), found a great incentive idea for her teen volunteers that she can do right in her hospital: She offers quarterly tours to junior volunteers who show up for 75 percent or more of the shifts they are required to have.

Since offering the tours, she's seen teens' volunteer hours increase by 14 percent.

That's because these aren't just any tours. No one else gets to see what these junior volunteers do, not visitors and not other volunteers, Krueger says.

"We really wanted it to be just their reward," says Krueger. Meaning while other tours may show the morgue, they don't get into the detail the incentive tours do, like visiting the lab too and examining body parts.

Teen tours have also included watching surgeries and visiting the helipad during a take-off or landing.

"We picked certain areas we knew would be interesting, things people normally don't get to see," she says.

The logistics were pretty easy to work out, she says. Since all hospital volunteers go through HIPAA patient confidentiality training and infection control education, it was really just about going to each department to work out the details. For instance, only six people are allowed on the helipad at a time. Since there are around 20 volunteers per tour, she split the one group into three.

Krueger says she has a dedicated group of junior volunteers whose interests lie in the medical field and who always put in their hours (12 a month during the school year, 20 a month in the summer). But, she notes, a full 50 percent of her volunteers are new to the tour every quarter.

Source: Amy Krueger, Junior Volunteer Assistant, Director, Volunteer Services, St. Cloud Hospital, St. Cloud, MN. Phone (320) 255-5638. E-mail: riedemanj@centracare.com

Volunteer Teams? Let the Fun Begin!

Whenever you have projects that allow for teams of volunteers, the participants are set to have fun. That's a great advantage of the team concept.

Here are a few doses of fun you can inject into any team effort:

1. To keep volunteers motivated throughout the duration of a long project, award increasingly attractive prizes for higher levels of team accomplishment.

2. Whatever the volunteer project, decide on some record-setting goal volunteer teams can set out to break — contributed hours, number of people served, calls made, cans or bags of donated items collected.

3. If you have a project or event that involves speed, give several chips to each team. The object is for each team to get rid of their chips, so each time the team completes a task, they get to discard one of their chips. The first team to get rid of all their chips wins.

Creative Gifts to Motivate Volunteers

The John Ball Zoo (Grand Rapids, MI), employs a variety of ways to thank their volunteers. One of their favorites? Inexpensive gifts.

Working with a company connected with a variety of product vendors the zoo is able to give their volunteers:

1. **Theme gifts** relating to the zoo's seasonal theme or current focus, such as kangaroo pins when Australia was in the spotlight, and a mini cooler with the zoo logo.

2. **Christmas mementos.** For Christmas, each volunteer was given a bookmark embedded with flower seeds — forget-me-nots — that they could plant in spring as reminders that the zoo would "forget them not."

3. **Good work tokens.** When volunteers are seen doing a good job, they are handed coupons for soda, popcorn or ice cream at the zoo concession stand.

Source: John Ball Zoo, Grand Rapids, MI. Phone (616) 336-4301.

Youth Volunteers: How to Recruit, Train, Motivate and Reward Young Volunteers

PERKS THAT BENEFIT YOUTH

What an adult may perceive as a benefit of volunteering and what a young person perceives as benefits are two different things. Even different ages among youth will require different kinds of benefits as a means to convince them to volunteer or as an incentive to keep them involved over time. This chapter will explore some of the perks to consider when working with young volunteers.

Point Out All of Volunteering's Benefits

People volunteer for different reasons. That's why it's important that your recruitment literature points out all of volunteering's benefits. Review your volunteer recruitment information. Make sure it mentions that volunteering allows an individual to:

✓ Favorably impact a community's quality of life.
✓ Gain recognition.
✓ Learn or develop skills.
✓ Receive free or discounted perks.
✓ Gain work experience.
✓ Strengthen leadership skills.
✓ Socialize.
✓ Build self-esteem and confidence.
✓ Meet new people.
✓ Enjoy cultural, educational and/or recreational opportunities.
✓ Feel needed and valued.
✓ Make a difference in someone's life.
✓ Express gratitude for help received in the past from an organization.

Think Creatively When It Comes to Volunteer Perks

Giving your volunteers little perks goes a long way for recruitment, retention and motivation. Coming up with ideas that are unique to your organization, or giving volunteers the same benefits as staff, helps them feel connected to your organization and that they're truly part of your team.

Healthcare organizations can offer:

- Free flu shots or immunizations.
- Massage therapy discounts — staff rates.
- Wellness center or gym discounts — staff rates.
- Cafeteria discounts.
- Free parking.
- Attendance to lectures and training.
- Pharmacy discounts.

Organizations involved in the arts can offer:

- Free tickets to performances.
- Discounted tickets for family and friends.
- Special showings and/or backstage tours.
- Free memberships.
- Gift shop discounts.

Recreation organizations (e.g., zoos, parks, pools, etc. can offer:

- Free passes for volunteers, friends and family.
- Free bus and trolley tours.
- Special days when the doors are only open for volunteers and families so they can have the place to themselves.
- Special discounts/coupons no one else receives.

Source: Tammy Atherton, Director, Volunteer Services, Banner Mesa Medical Center, Mesa, AZ. Phone (480) 461-2200 ext. 3. E-mail: tammy.atherton@bannerhealth.com
Dede Fleisher, Director, Volunteer Services, Trinity Mother Frances Health System, Tyler, TX. Phone (903) 531-4435. E-mail: fleishd@tmfhs.org
Carolyn Williams, Volunteer Coordinator, Philharmonic Center for the Arts, Naples, FL. Phone (239) 254-2705. E-mail: cwilliams@thephil.org
Heather Triplett, Manager of Volunteer Services, Cleveland Metroparks, Cleveland, OH. Phone (216) 635-3258. E-mail: hat@clevelandmetroparks.com

Grants, Awards for Youth

Christopher Columbus Awards — Youth organizations and 6th, 7th and 8th graders eligible for this award. Students find an innovative solution to a community problem. Winners receive all-expense-paid, one-week trip to Epcot at Walt Disney World; $25,000 community grant from the Columbus Foundation to develop their idea in their community; and a $2,000 savings bonds for each student. Entry deadline: Feb. 8, 2010.

For more info: The National Science Foundation. Phone (800) 291-6020 Website: www.christophercolumbusawards.com

Colgate's Youth for America Award — Awards of $100 to $2,000 to groups with the most creative, successful projects. Colgate is especially interested in Boy/Girl Scouts, Boys and Girls Clubs, Camp Fire Girls, Girls, Inc., and 4-H Clubs, although all groups are eligible for more than 300 cash awards.

For more info: David Forman, Colgate's Youth for America Award , PO Box 1058, FDR Station, New York, NY 10150-1058. Phone (212) 736-0564. E-mail: fcw001@aol.com. Website: www.colgate.com

PERKS THAT BENEFIT YOUTH

Encourage Young Volunteers with 'Job Training' Options

Do you know of teenagers who would benefit from volunteering, but you're not quite sure how to pitch the opportunity?

Hit them in their wallets.

Teens seeking their first job often face the problem of having little or no experience. Your hook? Emphasizing how volunteering can provide just the experience they need to fill out that job application.

Here are possible volunteer posts that would look good on a job resume:

- ❑ Volunteer on an Adopt-a-Highway project.
- ❑ Offer babysitting services to adults so they may volunteer.
- ❑ Make calls for a local fundraising campaign.
- ❑ Help sort, shelve and bag groceries at the local food shelf.
- ❑ Serve food and/or wash dishes at a local soup kitchen.

- ❑ Read to residents at the local nursing home .
- ❑ Volunteer at a school tutoring a favorite subject or assisting the janitor.
- ❑ Help with the local Special Olympics.
- ❑ Hand out water or snacks at fundraising run/walk/bike events.
- ❑ Shelve books at the library.
- ❑ Walk dogs at the animal shelter.

Assist these young people further by helping them create their first resume. Include names of responsible adult supervisors as references. Have the teens learn yet another skill by approaching these adults to ask permission to use them as references and perhaps request a letter of recommendation.

Need further motivation? Realize that, through these efforts, you will be encouraging a lifetime of volunteerism.

Volunteering Aids Students in Future Career Choice

One way to market your youth volunteer program is to point out the potential benefits, especially hands-on training in a future career field.

Officials at Emerson Hospital (Concord, MA) are introducing teens to the medical field and working hard to set a higher standard when it comes to student volunteering.

Sharon Knox, director of community services, says the hospital makes its program more involved in the hopes of getting volunteers interested in the medical field, especially nursing since the country is facing a shortage of nurses.

The student volunteer program at Emerson Hospital is a little more rigorous than many. Each youth is asked to contribute at least a 100 hours of volunteer service per year. But along with those extra hours comes valuable hands-on experience.

"It's not like some other hospitals where the volunteer program consists of students filing papers all day or doing menial jobs. Emerson spends a lot of time training students to be able to work with patients in transporting them," says Alyssa Bowie, a former volunteer.

Bowie is now enrolled in the nursing program at the University of Connecticut. While she always wanted to go into the medical field, volunteering at Emerson gave her something more.

"I wouldn't say Emerson was what made me decide I wanted to go into nursing, but it gave me exposure to the different fields of nursing out there," she says.

Bowie says the youth volunteer program at Emerson Hospital showed her the very basics of medical care. Besides working in the gift shop and transport, volunteers learn how to hook up someone's oxygen or tell how full the tank is, how to hook up other machines, how to know when an IV is dry and so on.

Emerson has a large student volunteer program with 148 students this year. Last year students logged 13,855 hours of community service.

Sources: Sharon Knox, Director Community Services, and Alyssa Bowie, Student Volunteer, Emerson Hospital, Concord, MA. Phone (978) 287-3201.
E-mail: sknox@emersonhosp.org;
Alyssa.bowie@huskymail.uconn.edu

Provide Volunteers With Proof of Service

Young people volunteer for many reasons. Some do so because they wish to include the experience on their college entrance forms, others because they want to include it on their resume when applying for a job. Volunteering shows a positive character trait that colleges and universities, as well as employers, are looking for. Here's one way to help your volunteers by creating tangible proof of their volunteering activities:

Have your local newspaper print a group photo at volunteer activity sites. During your organization's volunteer recognition event, present each person in the photo a copy of the print along with a Certificate of Appreciation signed by your organization's board members and/or the recipient of the volunteer effort. This way, the volunteer receives press coverage, a photo and a certificate as well as being recognized publicly for his/her efforts.

PERKS THAT BENEFIT YOUTH

Reference Letter Is Powerful Tool in Job Search

As young people prepare to make the transition from school to the workplace, they can gain enormous advantages from volunteering. Giving their time and effort provides them not only with opportunities for personal growth, but also with practical work experience and skills development.

As a volunteer manager, you may be asked to provide a letter of reference (see sample at right) for a young person. A reference letter summarizes the responsibilities carried out by the volunteer and assesses how effective the volunteer was in fulfilling those duties.

If you provide details on the skills that were polished or picked up in the position, this will be a more powerful tool for your youth volunteers in their future job searches.

University Program Provides Extra Incentive for Student Volunteers

The Students in Service (SIS) program provides an extra incentive to college-age volunteers, and nonprofit organizations get to reap the benefits.

Campuses across Washington, California, Hawaii, Montana, Idaho, Oregon and soon Alaska, take part in the program.

SIS, administered through Washington Campus Compact (Bellingham, WA), gives qualifying students a monetary award for serving their community. The awards, funded by the Corporation for National and Community Service, are put towards tuition and student loans in the following amounts:

- 300 hours of service = $1,000
- 450 hours of service = $1,250
- 900 hours of service = $2,362

Patrick McGinty, program director, SIS, says the awards are noncompetitive and 2,000 slots are open every year to students. Once students apply for the program, and their applications are approved, they are guaranteed an award if they fulfill their term of service commitment.

McGinty says the program is attractive to young people since many students must work to help pay for rising tuition costs and while SIS doesn't compete with the private sector, the award helps keep students volunteering, too.

SIS staff works with participating campuses that are Campus Compact members. A student picks a volunteer opportunity (SIS does not do volunteer placement) and applies to enroll in the program.

The coordinating nonprofit organization must also sign a site supervisor agreement.

The student agrees to volunteer 300, 450 or 900 hours for said nonprofit, (McGinty says most choose 300 or 900), and the nonprofit agrees to sign the monthly time log,

December 15, 2009

Jane Smith
ABC Children's Theatre
Anytown, USA 12345

Dear Ms. Smith:

This letter is a personal recommendation for Melissa Styles. Melissa has been a member of the New City Children's Drama Workshop for the past three years. During that time, I have come to know Melissa very well.

Melissa has been actively involved in our youth volunteer program. She has made a fine contribution to the organization and has assisted in several full-scale productions at the Regency Theatre and numerous recitals over the years. When Melissa began studying theatre at her college, she showed a real enthusiasm for her studies. Using the skills she was learning in school, she became a production assistant for our organization. Her dance background, stage experience and ability to work with children made our productions far more successful than we had anticipated.

I believe Melissa's excellent character and her desire to succeed in her chosen career will make her an excellent employee.

Sincerely,

Tammy Jones
Volunteer Coordinator

supervise and train the volunteer. Students get one year to complete 300 or 450 hours and two years to complete 900 hours.

Fifty-one percent of the student's volunteer time must be in the form of direct service.

McGinty says many SIS volunteers pick opportunities based on their academic interests and career goals. There are mentors, counselors, nursing and environmental volunteers.

SIS is a win for both the students and the communities.

Brian Heinrich, director of communications, says because SIS offers an award, more students step up to volunteer, helping with recruitment. And, because the students must fulfill either a 300- or 900-hour commitment, they stay longer with the organization, helping retention rates and saving training resources.

McGinty says the SIS program is marketed to college academic departments and financial aid offices, and volunteer centers as well as community organizations.

To find a Campus Compact Partner in your area, go to www.studentsinservice.org. This site also has guidelines for site supervisors and information on becoming part of Campus Compact.

Sources: Patrick McGinty, Program Director, Students in Service Program, Washington Campus Compact, Bellingham, WA. Phone (360) 650-7257. E-mail: patrick.mcginty@wwu.edu. Website: www.studentsinservice.org
Brian Heinrich, Director of Communications, Washington Campus Compact, Bellingham, WA. Phone (360) 650-4147. E-mail: brian.heinrich@wwu.edu

Youth Volunteers: How to Recruit, Train, Motivate and Reward Young Volunteers

MATCHING YOUTH WITH APPROPRIATE TASKS

Satisfying young peoples' volunteer interests while providing them with rewarding experiences requires balance. Begin by making an earnest effort to understand your volunteers' interests. What do each of them enjoy doing? What are their hobbies? What's driving them to want to volunteer? Once you understand that to some degree, you can begin to match them with appropriate projects and job responsibilities.

Balance Youth's Likes With Enrichment Experiences

As you involve young people in volunteer experiences, be mindful of providing them with the right mix of opportunities they find rewarding along with those that will enrich and nurture them as maturing volunteers. To get that proper mix, follow these steps:

1. Learn their personal interests and aptitudes. When youth first come on as volunteers, take extra care to provide a work experience they will find rewarding.

2. Monitor them more closely in the beginning. Do they feel their work is of value? Do they appear enthused or bored? What can you do to make them feel their work is more worthwhile?

3. Teach them what it's all about. Share real-life examples of why their service is needed, how they can make a difference in the lives of those you serve.

Using Youth for Special Events Volunteering

Seeking youth to volunteer? Take a cue from the Woburn Senior Center (Woburn, MA), where Judy Tanner, coordinator of programs and volunteers, reaches out to youth groups to fill volunteer needs for special events and a volunteer recognition.

Tanner says doing so works well for several reasons, including:

1. Special events fit into the schedules of youth volunteers more easily than a regular volunteer position.

2. By working in groups, volunteers get to work with friends.

3. Adult group leaders who usually come along help guide and supervise them.

4. Special event volunteering gives youth an opportunity to get involved with the community and possibly spark a lifelong interest in volunteering.

5. Using youth volunteers to help with a recognition event frees up Tanner's senior volunteers to truly enjoy their day.

When a special event comes up, Tanner contacts established youth groups — some church based, others community based. She meets with the group leader to work out details such as number of volunteers needed, for what duties, and for how long.

For example, youth volunteers from four groups helped at the annual volunteer appreciation event, Volunteers Help Our Senior Center Grow. They helped pick the theme, make decorations, decorate the hall, and act as greeters, servers and cleanup crew. "It gave senior volunteers a chance to feel appreciated," says Tanner.

She usually works with high schoolers but has had luck with all age groups, even 5- and 6-year-olds who can make posters and fliers for some of the special events.

Source: Judy Tanner, Programs/Volunteers, Woburn Council on Aging, Woburn, MA. Phone (781) 937-7899.
E-mail: judy2.1@netzero.net

MATCHING YOUTH WITH APPROPRIATE TASKS

Survey of Personal Interests Uncovers Special Opportunities

Are you aware of your volunteers' hobbies and special interests? How much do you know about those interests?

It's worth your time to learn more about each of your volunteers' special interests. Who knows when your awareness of a particular interest may be somehow used for volunteer purposes? Someone who collects butterflies, for instance, might be asked to give a presentation about the collection. Likewise, a volunteer who is into photography may be the perfect individual to take candid shots at an upcoming event. You never know where opportunities may arise to make use of volunteers' special interests.

To get more familiar with the hobbies and particular interests of your volunteers, invite them to complete a personal interests survey that you can keep on file. Depending on the number of volunteers with whom you work, you may even choose to create an index of interest categories that can be easily reviewed when a particular task calls for a certain set of interests.

Knowing your volunteers' special interests not only allows you to better match them with projects and tasks, but it has other benefits as well: Depending on their particular hobby, you can recognize individual volunteers weekly or monthly by having a display of their collection for others to see. Those whose hobbies are being showcased will be flattered and feel more appreciated than ever.

Special Interests, Hobbies Inventory

Name _____ Phone _____

Date Completed _____ E-mail _____

I would like to share with you my top special interests or hobbies. They include the following:

Special Interest/Hobby No. 1 _____
_____

Description of my interest/hobby _____
_____

How long I have been doing it: _____
_____

How I got started: _____
_____

Why I enjoy it: _____
_____

Any features about my hobby/interest/collection worth mentioning: _____
_____

Special Interest/Hobby No. 2 _____
_____

Description of my interest/hobby _____
_____

How long I have been doing it: _____
_____

How I got started: _____
_____

Why I enjoy it: _____
_____

Any features about my hobby/interest/collection worth mentioning: _____
_____

Discover your young volunteers' hobbies to learn more about them and what motivates them.

Ambassador Program Introduces Students to Health Fields

Sparking students' interest in healthcare and helping them make an informed decision about their desired career path are the main goals of a Student Ambassador Program at Provena Saint Joseph Medical Center (Joliet, IL).

The program allows high school students, age 15 and up, to volunteer and shadow in a hospital department for seven weeks.

Shannon Morgan, manager of volunteer services, says the program has benefited both students and staff. Not only does the program give students networking opportunities and written recommendations, it also provides staff with an extra pair of hands from an interested volunteer.

Morgan started the program from scratch on the advice and support of the hospital's CEO, Jeff Brickman, one of the key people involved in the program's success.

Here's how it works:

- Morgan worked with the district's superintendent and assistant superintendent to recruit area high school students. Counselors help identify which students have an interest in healthcare, based on course work and college goals, and give students the initial paperwork. The forms include references, parental consent and a doctor's note to make sure there are no health risks.

- Morgan interviews each student to determine who is serious about volunteering and truly interested in being there. Students rank their top three department choices and preferred day of week. Each student volunteers one day a week for five hours. Twenty-seven students are chosen to go through hospital orientation.

- Departments are selected based on their history of using volunteers, the quality of shadowing opportunities and the interest of students. Departments that express interest receive a presentation on the ambassador program, including suggestions on jobs students could perform, how to manage the students and how to welcome the students. For example, one of Morgan's ideas was asking a dedicated department member to step up and run the program.

- Departments are in charge of writing the job descriptions and providing any training. For example, Imaging and Radiology students mainly shadow, but nursing units' students are put to work filling water glasses, making beds and running errands. Students stay in one department from the beginning to the end of the program. Several departments let students rotate within their department, going from inpatient therapy to occupational therapy.

- At the end of the program, student and staff members fill out a survey detailing what worked and what could be different for the next year. A recognition event is held for students, their parents and staff. Students receive certificates of completion and a letter of recommendation for college. There are also staff-nominated awards for ambassadors. Staff receives an 8 X 10-inch certificate of thanks signed by the students, which can be hung in their department.

Source: Shannon Morgan, Manager, Volunteer Services, Provena Saint Joseph Medical Center, Joliet, IL. Phone (815) 725-7133, ext. 3466. E-mail: Shannon.morgan@provena.org

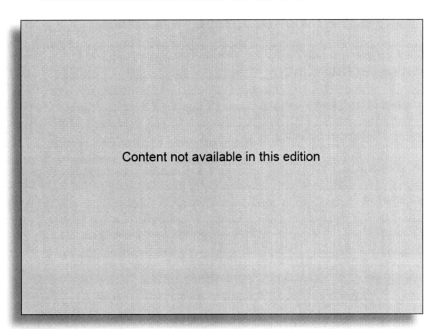
Content not available in this edition

Volunteers at Avera Sacred Heart (Yankton, SD) use this form to track required training at a combined competency fair/recognition luncheon.

MATCHING YOUTH WITH APPROPRIATE TASKS

Service Learning Projects Bring in Student Volunteers

The prospect of offering student service learning projects — in which high school students volunteer to fulfill class requirements — brings many questions.

For instance, what will students be capable of doing? How much supervision will they need? Will this make more work than it is worth?

Kathleen Pengelly, staffing coordinator, Lifeworks Services Inc. (Mendota Heights, MN) — which provides services to developmentally disabled adults — says she had apprehensions when asked by local high school representatives if Lifeworks could become a site for Spectrum, their service learning program.

Pengelly agreed to give it a try, and now seven years later, finds all her apprehensions were unfounded as the partnership is working out great.

The students, who must meet certain criteria to be involved, have been dedicated volunteers. Many have come back to work as paid staff and, with their families, have become donors.

Student volunteers serve one afternoon a week, working seamlessly with regular volunteers and staff, she says.

Pengelly details the program:

- **Staffing coordinator's role:** Pengelly creates a menu of volunteer opportunities based on client suggestions. (For example, one client wanted to open a coffee shop, so students helped her convert a space at the organization and make coffee.) Pengelly goes over a checklist with students that includes issues such as treating clients with respect, confidentiality, etc., and trains them (just as she does with regular volunteers).

- **School's role:** The program advisor provides students with the menu of opportunities. Students select an organization (Lifeworks is just one of many) where they wish to volunteer. The advisor sets up the assignments. Students keep journals to share with class. Advisor takes care of course requirements and any attendance or disciplinary problems.

Source: Kathleen Pengelly, Staffing Coordinator, Lifeworks Services, Inc., Mendota Heights, MN.
Phone (651) 365-3720. E-mail: kpengelly@lifeworks.org

Call on Youth to Teach Seniors

If your organization serves senior citizens who would like to get more comfortable with a computer, why not call on youth volunteers to help close the digital divide?

As adept as today's youth are at social networking, they make the perfect teachers for older adults who could benefit from learning even basic computer skills. Willing youth volunteers could teach older adults how to:

- ✓ Explore their interests on the Internet: genealogy, travel, history, hobbies and more.
- ✓ Write, send and receive e-mail messages to and from friends and loved ones.

- ✓ Produce and print a Microsoft Word document.
- ✓ Operate their digital camera, upload, print, view and e-mail photos.
- ✓ Join in an online social networking site such as Facebook (www.facebook.com).

Many older adults have no idea what they are missing because no one has ever shown them the available online wonders. And what gratification a young person would receive by teaching these basic skills!

Match Career Goals With Jobs That Need Attention

Your recruitment efforts will produce better results if you spend time up front matching volunteer candidates to specific job opportunities. Narrowing your search to a specific group (based on age, interests, etc.), will add another level of improved results.

If, for instance, you have selected college/university students as a target group, you can work within that group to match interests/skills with available job opportunities. Identify a list of job opportunities and then recruit based on students' majors and internship opportunities that specific volunteer jobs might offer.

Here are some examples:

- A **mass communications** or **journalism major** can contribute to your organization's newsletter.

- A **sociology** or **social work major** might assist in some capacity with clients.

- Get some extra assistance with financial reports from an **accounting major**.

You'll find any number of matching opportunities may exist — perhaps some with internship opportunities — if you take the time to narrow your search before you begin to recruit.

MATCHING YOUTH WITH APPROPRIATE TASKS

Foster Career Aspirations While Tackling Boredom, Turnover

Involving youth volunteers in all aspects of your organization can reduce any boredom they may experience and help them find satisfaction in helping out your program.

Staff at Deaconess Medical Center and Valley Hospital and Medical Center (Spokane, WA) — a multi-service healthcare system providing inpatient and outpatient services — work extensively with high school and college volunteers to match them with roles closely related to their career aspirations and capture their ongoing drive to volunteer.

At the beginning of each student session, employees welcome a new group of some 75 students to assist in day-to-day healthcare tasks and shadow them while on the job. Students are permitted direct access to emergency rooms and, in a highly supervised and controlled way, operating viewing rooms.

Joey Frost, director of volunteer services, says working with student volunteers in this program requires more time, but results in a more committed, engaged volunteer.

In the job shadow program, volunteers paired with staffers in their chosen field see everything employees see, as long as patients and doctors consent. Job shadowing areas include emergency/trauma, labor and delivery, surgery, radiology and more.

Volunteers are also encouraged to observe medical procedures in their department during their volunteer shift, says Frost, noting: "This tends to reduce the monotony of everyday duties by allowing them to observe and learn more about the procedures offered by our facility."

To help ensure successful placement, Frost notes that they carefully evaluate a young volunteer's maturity level and personal interests. In the past year at Deaconess Medical Center alone, 61 percent of junior, student and college volunteers continued volunteering at the healthcare facility after their initial term expired or took a leave of absence with the intention of returning in the near future to the volunteer program.

Most volunteers at the healthcare system begin their efforts in a non-patient care area and are allowed to switch departments in the next rotation. As a result of this flexibility, Frost says one junior volunteer has worked in multiple areas including pastoral care, patient care, gift shop and library service and emergency room.

Source: Joey Frost, Director of Volunteer Services; Jennifer Tucker, Volunteer Coordinator, Deaconess Medical Center and Valley Hospital and Medical Center, Spokane, WA. Phone (509) 473-3767. E-mail: FrostJ@Empirehealth.org

Special-needs Students Contribute to Program Success

What started as a student's desire to volunteer at her local hospital has snowballed into a full-fledged volunteer program for students with special needs.

Staff at Alliance Community Hospital (Alliance, OH) now work with 20 area students with disabilities who function effectively in their roles as volunteers within the hospital.

For the past year, working with autistic, physically and cognitively challenged students has been a blessing for the hospital and its staff, says Marcy Todd, volunteer coordinator. Todd says these student volunteers fill roles within the hospital's print shop, assemble IV kits, provide clerical assistance, help with patient registration and more.

Todd shares suggestions for creating a successful volunteer program for persons with special needs:

- E-mail staff to solicit ideas as to which areas the volunteers would most benefit your organization.

- Work with the volunteer's teachers, parents and job coaches to determine suitable roles and roles that offer the most possibility for success.

- Treat these volunteers as you would any other volunteer. Ask them to complete an application, provide them with thorough orientation and training and give them identification badges, uniforms and any other items other volunteers receive.

- Train with patience, but don't be afraid to request changes in how the students are performing. Todd has found that these student volunteers are anxious to perform well and are more than willing to adjust performance as needed.

"These volunteers are a very grateful and gracious group and a valuable asset," says Todd. "I would encourage everyone to take a look at implementing a students with disabilities volunteer program as it builds self esteem, they get the job done and they work hard to do it right."

Source: Marcy Todd, Volunteer Coordinator, Alliance Community Hospital, Alliance, OH. Phone (330) 596-7821. E-mail: mtodd@achosp.org

MATCHING YOUTH WITH APPROPRIATE TASKS

Targeted Guide Gets Students Involved in Meaningful Way

It seems nearly every high school and college has a service requirement for its students. If your organization has volunteering opportunities appropriate for young people, be sure and connect the dots from their requirements to your organization's door.

To streamline the connection between young people and volunteering tasks, the staff at the Animal Protective Foundation (Scotia, NY) created the guide, "For Kids Who Want to Help Homeless Pets."

Printed on an 8.5-by-11-inch paper so it can easily be produced in-house, the guide lists 11 opportunities for young people to help the organization, along with a list of websites for more information and a wish list of items the shelter currently needs.

Ways to get involved include making cat mats, forming an awareness club, organizing an awareness week and sponsoring a speaker from the foundation. Each tip also includes information to get started, such as instructions for how to make a cat mat or a link to a website for tips on how to start a club.

This communications tool both simplifies the process for young people to fulfill needed service tasks for the organization and reduces the staff time needed to help young people determine how they can serve the foundation in a meaningful way.

Source: Animal Protective Foundation, Scotia, NY. Phone (518) 374-3944.

Studies Indicate Child Volunteers Pursue Volunteerism into Adulthood

Study after study suggests the earlier you introduce kids to volunteering, the more likely they'll stay with it. Group activities are a good start for kids.

When Todd Madigan, community involvement coordinator at Sacred Heart Community Service (San Jose, CA), engages volunteers under 12, he puts them in group activities with a chaperone.

"We believe (group activities) not only add to the connection of the group itself, but also add something to the experience they have here. For example, serving the poor in the community is more powerful than doing it on one's own. These types of group activities are always simple and fun for kids; fun partly because they are with their friends, and partly because of their novelty," he says.

Some activities have included:

- Breaking down food into family-sized portions.

- Preparing bags of dried or canned goods.

- Sorting through donated clothes; weeding out stained, torn and unsuitable items.

- Putting donated clothes on hangers.

- Helping during the holidays and with events.

Madigan says, for him, focusing on a job description for this age isn't as important as letting the kids understand the significance of what they are doing and making sure they have a good

experience while they are there.

Source: Todd Madigan, Community Involvement Coordinator, Sacred Heart Community Service, San Jose, CA. Phone (408) 278-2180. E-mail: toddm@sacredheartcommunityservice.org

Supervising Younger Volunteers

One fact to consider when engaging volunteers under 12 is the need for supervision.

When Madigan works with groups of volunteers under 12, there is always a chaperone. He has specific rules each chaperone must follow:

✓ Chaperones should have a list of names and emergency phone numbers for every student in the group.

✓ Chaperones should be aware of SHCS's mission and the type of work students will be doing.

✓ Chaperones are expected to stay on site with the students at all times.

✓ Chaperones should know where each student in the group is located at all times.

✓ Chaperones are in charge of communicating and enforcing behavioral expectations, which include: listening carefully to staff instructions; staying on task; being cooperative; being polite and respectful to customers and staff; not leaving job area without permission; using appropriate language.

Youth Volunteers: How to Recruit, Train, Motivate and Reward Young Volunteers

VOLUNTEERING AS A FAMILY

There are all kinds of benefits for families who volunteer. It's a richly rewarding experience. And children who volunteer with their family are much more likely to begin volunteering on their own, even as a youngster. This chapter focuses what you can do to recruit, manage and make the most of family volunteering experiences for your organization.

Positions Help Recruit Family Volunteers

What is the best way to recruit volunteers who want to serve as a family? Two volunteer coordinators agree it's the position that brings the family volunteers to you. Positions that have no or a low age requirement, allow families to work together, require little commitment, occur during family-friendly times and have a measurable impact are key.

- Leah Forehand, volunteer coordinator, HomeBase Youth Services (Phoenix, AZ), schedules families with kids ages seven and older to volunteer for Chefs for a Night. The families prepare dinner for 25 youth residents.

  Forehand says a chef prepares the menu and ingredients and leaves easy-to-follow directions. "The families get to spend time together at the end of the day," says Forehand. "It's fun, simple and there is no long commitment." The families get to see exactly who they're helping and the youths are great at showing the families their appreciation, she says.

- Rachel Kesselman, director of volunteer services, Jewish Family and Children's Services (San Francisco, CA), says her holiday outreach positions have become a tradition for many families. During the four major Jewish holidays, families with school-age kids or younger fill gift bags and deliver them to those of the Jewish faith who are alone or isolated during the holidays.

  The bag assembling has become a full event — complete with snacks and an educational program for the kids the bags are helping. The volunteers fill 800 bags in two hours. Kesselman says it has been more work to organize the event, but the volunteers it brings to the organization are worth it. She says every year she has families who knock on her door to ask when the next event is and to make sure they're on the volunteer list.

When creating volunteer positions that appeal to families, Kesselman says to look at what you already offer. She has changed at least three positions to make them family friendly. For example, she took a traditional position of delivering meals to homebound HIV patients and re-marketed it for families. The opportunity not only offers family time, but gives kids a view into situations that might be foreign to them.

Source: Leah Forehand, Volunteer Coordinator, HomeBase Youth Services, Phoenix, AZ. Phone (602) 651-1804. E-mail: volunteer@hbys.org

Rachel Kesselman, Director, Volunteer Services, Jewish Family and Children's Services, San Francisco, CA. Phone (415) 449-1288. E-mail: rachelk@jfcs.org

---

Don't Forget the Power of the Internet

A great family-oriented volunteer position plays a major role in landing volunteer families. By using your website and the Internet, you can show families exactly what you have to offer.

Forehand says the best recruitment tool she uses to get family volunteers to check out her opportunities is the Internet.

Forehand saturates volunteer search engines (e.g., www.volunteermatch.org) with her opportunities. "Many of the tools are free and I use as many as possible," she says. The result of multiple postings is that your organization and family volunteering opportunities will easily pop up in search engines.

Gear Up for Family Volunteer Day

Have you made plans for Family Volunteer Day?

This annual day of service, held Nov. 20 (the Saturday before Thanksgiving), demonstrates the power of families who choose to volunteer together to support the communities in which they live and serve.

Family Volunteer Day — sponsored by HandsOn Network, generated by Points of Light Institute and The Walt Disney Company — offers an excellent opportunity to join hands and give back to your community in a meaningful way.

For more information, go to http://disney.go.com/disneyhand/familyvolunteers/

VOLUNTEERING AS A FAMILY

Benefits to Volunteering With Your Children

There are immeasurable benefits to volunteering with your children or grandchildren. You'll build the child's self-esteem as well as your own and foster a feeling of gratitude within the young person.

Here are some easy steps to beginning on the road to contributing to your community with children:

1. **Hold a tag sale for a cause.** Have children participate in cleaning and tagging the items for the sale and helping the day of the sale. Together, take the proceeds to your favorite local nonprofit and donate the leftovers to your local Goodwill or similar community agency.

2. **Visit a nursing home.** Elderly nursing home residents adore seeing children and if yours are old enough and willing, ask them to play a game or read to the residents. If your child/grandchild has a talent to share, such as playing piano or singing, this is a good time to share that talent.

3. **Conduct a food drive.** Local food shelves are particularly strapped with the changing economy and increase in need. Walk with your child through your neighborhood and ask neighbors to donate two canned items each. Together deliver the items to your local food shelf.

4. **Donate gently used toys.** Help your child sort through the toy box for outgrown or unwanted toys. Wash them and donate them to a local Head Start or low-income childcare.

5. **Pick up trash.** Bring two garbage bags on a walk to collect trash along the way. Use this opportunity to educate your child/grandchild about the effects of litter on the environment and value of recycling.

Offer Opportunities to Attract Family of Volunteers

If you're looking to welcome families as volunteers, put that information front and center in your volunteering brochure.

Content not available in this edition

Brenda J. Greenberg, director, volunteer services, Northern Services Group (Monsey, NY), intentionally uses pictures of families with young children in her recruitment brochure. Greenberg says she has had volunteers from age 2 to 100, and seeing intergenerational opportunities in the brochure draws people to volunteer.

By law, children under age 14 must be accompanied by a parent or guardian to volunteer at Northern Services Group. Greenberg makes that clear to parents when they call, telling them they cannot just drop off their young children, but that the agency does offer opportunities for parents and children to volunteer together. She also asks for a minimum commitment of 25 hours per year.

Nearly all opportunities in the brochure accommodate families. Greenberg also asks families for volunteering ideas.

Current opportunities for families include:

- Delivering food to homebound elderly.

- Being a friendly visitor to homebound elderly.

- Running a bingo game .

- Helping seniors do arts and crafts.

- Serving in the dining hall.

- Performing music or dances for the seniors.

- Transporting residents within the facility.

Source: Brenda J. Greenberg, Director Volunteer Services, Northern Services Group, Monsey, NY. Phone (845) 356-9880, ext. 241. E-mail: bgreenberg@northernservicesgroup.com

VOLUNTEERING AS A FAMILY

Offer All-in-the-family Volunteering Opportunities

Volunteering as a family is one way for volunteers to fulfill their giving commitments while teaching children giving values. Heather Jack, president, The Volunteer Family (Framingham, MA), has worked for more than five years matching family volunteers with worthy causes through The Volunteer Family website at www.thevolunteerfamily.org. Nearly 30,000 family volunteer opportunities are listed at the site to assist families in finding ways in which they can volunteer.

"Family volunteering helps nonprofit organizations broaden their services and their community outreach while improving public image and relations," says Jack.

One significant benefit for working with family volunteers is that bringing families on board to fill volunteer opportunities offers nonprofits the opportunity to bring young volunteers who offer energy, enthusiasm and a volunteer base for future, long-term volunteers.

"Working with volunteering families is a natural multiplier of volunteers for any nonprofit organization," Jack says. "And by working with youth, you are setting the basis for some potentially lifelong volunteers."

Training family volunteers requires a unique approach. Here are some important training tips for creating a beneficial family volunteer arrangement:

❑ Determine whether the family can participate in your organization's standard training schedule. If not, create training times that accommodate a family schedule.

❑ Consider creating a modified training session that accommodates families and the attention spans of younger volunteers. Conduct one-on-one training sessions per family as an ideal way to engage all family members during the training process.

❑ Create a handout or training manual that is brief and pointed, allowing families to review the information more thoroughly at home.

❑ Offer a family volunteer job description for their specific role within the organization and orientation geared specifically for this unique brand of volunteer group.

❑ Assign parents/guardians the role of leader so they organize their family unit as a volunteer entity. Assign one point person for all nonprofit communication.

❑ Recognize each individual in the family volunteer unit. Assign roles to each person within the family, outlining the specific roles and tasks they should complete. Clearly defined roles for each member allows the family to function better as a group.

❑ During the orientation, communicate to all family members, not only the adults. Communicate the organization's purpose and mission to youth as well as adults.

❑ Evaluate the organization's environment. Provide a safe, comfortable training and working environment conducive to family volunteer units.

❑ Find ways to recognize each individual for their contributions as well as thanking the family as a unit.

Source: Heather Jack, President, The Volunteer Family, Framingham, MA. Phone (508) 861-0560.
E-mail: hjack@thevolunteerfamily.org

Finding Families To Volunteer

Here are four ways to add families to your roll of valuable volunteers:

1. Distribute flyers at a local community event.

2. Blog about your opportunities at local family-oriented websites.

3. Be sure to prominently feature information about family volunteering opportunities on your website.

4. Ask families that currently volunteer to spread the word in their schools, neighborhoods, churches and synagogues.

How to Make the Most of Family Volunteers

Family volunteers are welcome at the Aquarium of the Pacific (Long Beach, CA), and benefits for doing so are great, says Sean Devereaux, manager of volunteer services.

Devereaux says family volunteering allows an organization to share its mission with young people. Additionally, an enthusiastic youth volunteer can share his or her knowledge and passion with others at the organization.

For families, Devereaux says: "This is an amazing opportunity to bond with your child while you are working toward a common goal. I think the experience is invaluable to families who participate, and it teaches important life lessons to the participating children."

Currently, 16 families volunteer at the aquarium. To maximize the benefits of family volunteering, Devereaux offers the following tips:

• "Be flexible and accommodating, but try to not dilute the core responsibilities of your volunteer positions.... A challenge is good."

• "Don't assume they can't do it. You will be surprised what they can accomplish."

• "Take everyone seriously — the parents and the children. We hold our volunteers to very high standards and family volunteers are no exception."

Source: Sean Devereaux, Manager of Volunteer Services, Aquarium of the Pacific, Long Beach, CA. Phone (562) 951-1672.
E-mail: sdevereaux@lbaop.org.
Website: www.aquariumofpacific.org

VOLUNTEERING AS A FAMILY

Enticing Siblings to Volunteer

Providing volunteer opportunities for siblings is a great way to involve and familiarize the next generation with volunteering.

Having family members volunteer together is rewarding to both the organization and the volunteers, says Heather Jack, president of The Volunteer Family (Framingham, MA). "Children feel valued, they develop new skills and siblings get to see each other in a different environment," says Jack, who started The Volunteer Family in 2003 to provide a link between volunteers and nonprofit organizations.

The possibilities are endless when it comes to providing volunteer opportunities for siblings, she says. Her organization has volunteer families help the homeless, the sick and disabled, the elderly, children, animals and the environment.

She offers 10 suggestions on ways siblings can volunteer together:

Content not available in this edition

1. Grow a vegetable garden. Donate produce to a food bank.
2. Read to a sick child.
3. Play board games or cards with nursing home residents.
4. Provide foster care for kittens and pups.
5. Help clean up a local river or park.
6. Teach computer skills.
7. Make welcome baskets for new Habitat for Humanity homeowners.
8. Help build playground equipment or bicycles.
9. Collect and donate old books and toys.
10. Help with a yard sale or bake sale.

Another benefit of bringing siblings in to volunteer? Since they don't usually run in the same social groups, Jack says, they have separate groups of friends to tap for additional volunteer opportunities. Check out www. thevolunteerfamily.org for more project ideas.

Source: Heather Jack, President, The Volunteer Family, Framingham, MA. Phone (508) 405-2220. E-mail: vfamily@res1mtg.com.

Help Youth See the Benefits of Family Volunteering

Time is such a valuable commodity that youth who may be willing to volunteer at a nonprofit may appear reluctant to do so for fear it will mean time away from their family. The solution? Promote the idea of volunteering as a family activity.

Here are some ideas to share with potential volunteer families:

• It allows youth the opportunity to share their values with their parents in a dynamic way.

• Volunteering as a family strengthens relationships by allowing family members to see one another in new settings and surroundings.

• It provides an opportunity for family members to be positive role models for siblings.

Volunteer families work together to gain insight into the challenges faced by others in their community, their society and throughout the world.

The Ties That Bind: Volunteering Brings Mother and Daughter Together

If you think all teens and parents do is squabble over curfews and clothes, consider Nita and Ashley Veracruz.

For the past three years, this mother/daughter pair has been volunteering with the Helping One Student To Succeed (HOSTS) Learning program in the Pasadena Independent School District (Pasadena, TX). For 30 minutes a day, one day a week, Ashley, a high school senior, tutors students at Williams Elementary School, where her mom, Nita, is a HOSTS Learning assistant.

Nita became involved with the program several years ago when Ashley's fourth grade teacher asked her to volunteer as a HOSTS Learning mentor. HOSTS Learning is a nationally recognized, structured program that pairs a student who needs help learning to read and write with a community member who wants to make a difference in a student's life.

"Working with the children, watching their confidence grow as their skills improve is really rewarding," says Nita, who has been with the HOSTS Learning program since its inception in the Pasadena Independent School District in the late 1990s. Her enthusiasm for the program eventually spread to her daughter.

Ashley, along with members of her high school volleyball team, spends time during the off-season tutoring students in grades 1 through 5 on subjects such as reading, writing and math.

"I like interacting with the kids," she says. "It's exciting to watch them learn and grow."

Thanks to the efforts of HOSTS Learning volunteers like Nita and Ashley, state test scores rose among students involved with the program that school year. More than 80 percent of students passed the fourth grade Texas Assessment of Academic Skills reading exam. Recent scores also show that more than 90 percent of HOSTS students passed their regular reading class with an average grade of 80.

Sources: Nita Veracruz, HOSTS Learning Assistant, and Ashley Veracruz, HOSTS Learning Mentor, Pasadena Independent School District, Pasadena, TX. Phone (713) 920-6800.

Family Volunteering Reinforces Ties

When asked about the benefits of volunteering as a family, participants in a recent study by the Center for Urban Policy and the Environment, Indiana University-Purdue University Indianapolis, identified several themes, including bringing the family closer together.

That finding holds true in the case of the Veracruz family of Pasadena, TX. Not only was mother Nita able to persuade daughter Ashley to become a HOSTS Learning mentor, but she also enlisted the help of her husband, son and parents. "It's a real family affair," says Nita.

For more information on "Family Volunteering: An Exploratory Study of the Impact on Families," a study conducted by the Center for Urban Policy and the Environment, School of Public and Environmental Affairs, Indiana University–Purdue University Indianapolis, visit: www.pointsoflight.org/pdfs/FamilyVolunteering.pdf.

Recognition Ideas for Family Volunteers

It only makes sense that families who volunteer together like to be recognized together. Heather Jack, president, The Volunteer Family (Framingham, MA), offers these ways to recognize families as a whole:

- Nominate the family for an award. National awards include the Presidential Volunteer Service Award (www. presidentialserviceawards.com), the Disney Family Fun Award (www.familyfun.com/volunteers) and the Angel Soft Million Family Service Pledge (www.angelsoft. com/angelsinaction). Many states and cities also have awards.

- Pitch the story about a family who has really taken an initiative to volunteer for your organization to your local paper. Have the family sign a photo release.

- Throw a family volunteer mixer so family volunteers can meet and mingle with each other.

- Give families a free dinner at a local family restaurant.

- Organize an outing that appeals to the entire family (e.g., picnic, ball game, pool party, ice cream social or children's theater tickets).

- Take pictures of each family as they volunteer and frame them as a gift.

- Ask families to walk in a parade on your behalf.

- Give families a free dinner at a local family restaurant.

- Name something after the family, such as a tree or flowerbed they planted for your organization.

However you choose to recognize your family volunteers, Jack suggests talking to them first to ensure they're okay with it, especially if you're planning to nominate them for awards or telling your local paper about them.

Source: Heather Jack, President, The Volunteer Family, Framingham, MA. Phone (508) 405-2220. E-mail: hjack@thevolunteerfamily.org

Youth Volunteers: How to Recruit, Train, Motivate and Reward Young Volunteers

MANAGEMENT ISSUES: TRAINING, CONFLICT AND MORE

Working with young and college-age volunteers requires different management approaches than adults. Whether you are dealing with conflict or managing a group project or working in a supervisory role, the management methods you use will impact the accomplishments of younger volunteers and their level of fulfillment. It's important to earn and maintain the trust of these young volunteers and to provide them with clearly defined goals and responsibilities.

Help Young Volunteers Hit the Ground Running

At the Kidzu Children's Museum (Chapel Hill, NC), learning is a hands-on adventure driven by a strong volunteer workforce.

This interactive museum for children and families has hosted a series of nationally recognized exhibits including Where the Wild Things Are and Mister Rogers' Neighborhood. In any given semester, at least 40 volunteers help with programs and assist the museum's 400 members.

Work-study students from the local college assist in staffing 90 percent of the museum's volunteer positions. Local high school students serve as volunteers to fulfill community service requirements.

These relationships create a win-win situation for the students and the museum, helping to create a volunteer base while providing the young volunteers with an opportunity to build their reference and resume file.

Tina Clossick, director of operations, shares some of the techniques she uses to help prepare the museum's young volunteers for their many tasks:

- **Training is key to the success of the volunteer.** The museum's traveling exhibits require ongoing training so volunteers become knowledgeable about each incoming exhibit. Volunteers receive one-hour trainings to learn the details of each new exhibit.

- **Teach early childhood techniques.** Volunteers learn "scaffolding" where they identify the ability of the child and help the child stretch his/her knowledge.

- **Model the behavior you would like student volunteers to emulate.** In training, Kidzu volunteers role-play to become efficient at techniques needed to work with young children and parents.

- **Train the volunteers to be supervisors but not disciplinarians.** The volunteer learns to keep the area safe for children and artful distraction techniques if a child misbehaves. Volunteers seek out caregivers for disciplinary needs.

- **Customer service is a critical component.** Like any other service-based organization, Kidzu requires strong customer service orientation from its volunteers. Volunteers are trained to not only answer a question, but to give more than requested by offering more details. For example, they not only point out where the restroom is, but explain that changing tables are available for little ones.

Clossick says she finds working with youth volunteers to be a great advantage as they are easy to work with and have high energy levels. Volunteers age 15 to 22 also tend to have flexible schedules, which is compatible with the museum's operations.

"You can learn as much from these volunteers as they learn from you," she notes.

Source: Tina Clossick, Director of Operations, Kidzu Museum, Chapel Hill, NC. Phone (919) 933-1455. E-mail: clossick@mindspring.com

Three Steps Improve Volunteer Success

The Kidzu Museum (Chapel Hill, NC) welcomes high school and college students for volunteering roles. But working with young people can pose some challenges, says Tina Clossick, director of operations.

Here, she offers three tips for helping young volunteers succeed:

1. If friends want to volunteer together, offer each a separate task to avoid talking and distraction.

2. Volunteers at Kidzu are required to call if they'll be more than 10 minutes late. Consistent tardiness can lead to dismissal, but Clossick assures reminders do the trick.

3. To avoid lackluster performance and keep young volunteers energized, give daily feedback and stress the positive. Offer constructive criticism, but also chat with volunteers one on one about their lives to create a warm, friendly atmosphere.

Youth Corps Training Develops Future Volunteers, Leaders

Engage young people in your volunteer corps and they may become volunteers for life.

Beginning a pilot program in 2008, staff with Midland Care (Topeka, KS) — an independent, not-for-profit community-based organization providing options to families with challenging health care needs — worked with 27 children of staff members and friends, ages 10 to 15, to educate them on becoming volunteers on the Midland campus.

Through three days of training in June, July and August, youth corps trainees learned extensive life skills that will assist both as Midland volunteers and in other capacities, says Suz McIver, director of volunteers.

"We set the kids up by the end of the summer to become volunteers on our campus," McIver says, adding: "Kids in this world bring a lot of fresh perspective. Our youth corps training not only enlarges our volunteer base, the kids benefit from it both personally and professionally."

McIver offers suggestions for implementing a teen training program:

❑ **Design a character-building program.** Focus on leadership skills, trust, effectiveness, communication and other skills that will help trainees become responsible volunteers and community members.

❑ **Keep training numbers small and focused.** Condense trainee spaces to a number that allows one-on-one training and individual attention.

❑ **Don't overscript training staff.** Ensure that your program allows for hands-on involvement and decision-making by the teen trainees and is flexible to the needs of each training group.

❑ **Don't underestimate how well teens can do under this type of a program.** Volunteers and staff at Midland Care found that their teen trainees appreciate the flexibility of being self-led.

The youth focused on five significant categories in determining rules and boundaries for the sessions: privacy, participation, conflict resolution, patient treatment and professional conduct. A fee of $25 per participant helped offset costs.

To share the success of this experience, Midland staff are creating a manual guiding other organizations in building a youth program. This manual will be available for purchase at www.midlandcareconnection.org in early 2010.

Source: Suz McIver, Director of Volunteers, Midland Care, Topeka, KS. Phone (785) 232-2044. E-mail: smciver@midlandcc.org

Goals Drive Youth Training

Staff at Midland Care (Topeka, KS) initiated a youth corps volunteer training program with the following goals in mind:

- To build and provide volunteer assistance at Midland Care.

- To teach compassion and the joy of selfless giving to youth.

- To listen to new ideas and fresh perspectives from youth volunteers.

- To offer an open learning environment in areas of gerontology, grief, loss and end of life.

- To offer youth companionship to Midland clients.

- To grow youth volunteers into adult volunteers.

- To orient, recognize and evaluate youth who participate in the program.

- To introduce youth to health-related careers.

Give Teens Their Own Volunteer Board

Provide teen volunteers with access to adult leadership roles. This unique approach will help attract bright and committed teens who remain with your volunteer program long-term.

JoAnne Burch Burris, volunteer coordinator, Cardinal Hill Rehabilitation Hospital (Lexington, KY), manages a Teen Board comprising high school juniors and seniors from central Kentucky.

The board meets monthly to brainstorm project ideas. Burch Burris serves as the session guide, rather than as a supervisor. "I want them to have ownership over their projects," she says. Projects include gift-wrapping, folding and stuffing, writing get-well notes and planning special events.

Board members must volunteer at the hospital a minimum of three hours monthly. The board meetings contribute one hour of that time.

District guidance counselors nominate board members. Each member fills out an application, which is reviewed by Burch Burris. There is no cap on the number of students selected. Juniors are automatically invited back for their senior year.

Source: JoAnne Burch Burris, Volunteer Coordinator, Cardinal Hill Rehabilitation Hospital, Lexington, KY. Phone (859) 254-5701 ext 5350. E-mail: jbb1@cardinalhill.org

How Can You Repair Trust With Your Teen Volunteers?

When a teen volunteer breaks your trust, repairing that trust can be difficult.

Judy Findlay, coordinator for the Teenaged Group Services (TAGS) program at Kishwaukee Community Hospital (Dekalb, IL), has worked with teens for 10 years. She says that when trust is broken, you have to look at each situation individually.

When problems arise Findlay tries to offer the volunteer a second chance. For example, for a minor problem like a dress code violation or having food at the reception desk, the teen receives a warning and a letter asking that the problem be corrected. If the problem continues, the teen is dropped from the program. Usually the verbal warning and letter correct the problem, says Findlay, noting that kids can be kids.

In severe situations such as a break in confidentiality, the volunteer is let go immediately. "There must be consequences for such actions," she says. "We have to know we can trust them."

Hospital officials try to get the right teens the first time through careful screening, orientation and 15 hours of training. Also, each teen must have a reference from a non-relative, such as a teacher or minister.

The only time when trust can't be repaired for a minor problem is when the teen doesn't want to be there in the first place, Findlay says. "When parents are pushing them to be here, then it's not a good situation."

Source: Judy Findlay, Coordinator, TAGS Program, Kishwaukee Community Hospital, Dekalb, IL.
Phone (815) 756-1521, ext. 3373.
E-mail: voloffice@kishhospital.org

Content not available in this edition

MANAGEMENT ISSUES: TRAINING, CONFLICT AND MORE

Tips for Working With First-time Offender Youth Volunteers

Filling volunteer positions with youth seems like a natural extension for nonprofits, but working with first-time youth offenders may give some organizations reason for pause.

One group finding success working with this special population is Man in the Mirror (Casselberry, FL), a Christian ministry nonprofit organization.

Working with Florida's state Parole Alternatives for Youth (P.A.Y.) program, first-time offenders ages 14 to 22 fill data entry and warehouse positions alongside other youth volunteers in a school-sponsored Bright Futures program for high-achieving students to secure college scholarships. P.A.Y. volunteers work 20 to 40 hours over 90 days.

In 2008, Man in the Mirror worked with around 120 young first-time offenders.

Employees are not told which students are from the offender program and which from the Bright Futures program, giving all youth the same footing.

Students must call on their own to interview for the position and not have a parent do so, Mayer notes. Students who are accepted for the experience learn important career skills and can earn a letter of recommendation for future employment.

Source: Daphne Mayer, Volunteer Coordinator, Man in the Mirror, Casselberry, FL. Phone (407) 472-2115.
E-mail: daphnemayer@maninthemirror.org

Going Paperless Makes Teen Orientation Run Smoother

Think about how much paper your volunteer office uses for each volunteer: application forms, volunteer handbooks, guidelines, orientation materials, etc. Now think about how much of that information could be put online.

That's exactly what Jamine Hamner, coordinator of volunteer services, Saint Joseph Health Care (Lexington, KY) did. A year ago Hamner and her staff wanted to streamline the teen volunteer program from a two-day orientation to a two-hour orientation.

What they did was create a paperless office with an online application system that works for the entire volunteer program.

A volunteer can search the available opportunities, complete and submit the application directly online. The applicant then receives an e-mail with instructions to complete the orientation online. The orientation materials — a confidentiality agreement, multiple choice safety test, multiple choice HIPAA test, volunteer agreement and orientation checklist — are all completed online and signed by the volunteer electronicly. As the applicant submits each item, it goes to Hamner's e-mail. She calls the volunteer and sets up an interview. During the interview she gets the required background information and finishes up the orientation process. Once the volunteer begins placement, each has their own login and password to check schedules and updates.

One of the biggest advantages to going paperless is the lack of wait time a volunteer has between applying and starting. Before going paperless, Hamner says, the application process took about one month, depending on if the volunteer signed up right after the monthly orientation. Now the process takes a week.

Hamner admits the office isn't entirely paperless. They do mail paper copies of forms to volunteers when needed — about one every three months. Hamner still requires one ink-to-paper signature for the parental consent form for the teen volunteer program, which is accessible from the website.

Source: Jamine Hamner, Coordinator of Volunteer Services, Saint Joseph Health Care, Lexington, KY. Phone (859) 313-1290.
E-mail: hamnerja@sjhlex.org

Advice for Setting Up Paperless Office

Jamine Hamner, coordinator of volunteer services, Saint Joseph Health Care (Lexington, KY) says her office went paperless through trial and error. Now, that she's done it, Hamner says she'd never go back.

Hamner offers a list of essentials an organization must have when converting to a paperless office:

- Internet connection from your work computer.
- A Web site that allow you to upload documents.
- Your documents in an electronic format (e.g., Word or PDF) that will be accessible.
- An online volunteer application that can be submitted from the Web site.
- Orientation forms, agreements, tests which can be created through your Web site.
- A separate place to store your electronic volunteer files, such as your organization's server or online file storage.
- A scanner with an automatic document feeder.

Hamner says before pursuing a paperless office it's important to ask your IT department if your Web site can support the transition. If not, Hamner says, by using a search engine organizations should be able to locate free and inexpensive options to create their own paperless office.

Put the Kibosh on Gossip

What can you do to eliminate, or at least diminish, volunteer gossip in your organization?

Beth Bloomfield, director, Retired and Senior Volunteer Program, Volunteer Center Orange County (Santa Ana, CA), says a written gossip policy should be mandatory.

"A written policy should lay out a definition of gossip and the consequences of gossiping," says Bloomfield. "The policy may be created by your board of directors, senior staff, HR department or a volunteer manager may even wish to create the policy in partnership with their volunteers."

Bloomfield says avoiding the problem because a volunteer manager is unprepared and uncomfortable addressing gossip may be harmful. "Gossip can undermine morale, affect productivity and sometimes even lead to the loss of volunteers. If volunteers are not taught by their supervisor to effectively handle gossip, it could affect a volunteer's creativity and commitment to the organization they serve."

Bloomfield offers these tips when dealing with gossip among volunteers:

1. **Don't gossip yourself.**

2. **Curb others who gossip and promote peer responsibility to do the same.**

3. **Decide how you will address gossip.** During a training exercise practice these responses one may ask the gossiper: Is this confidential? Why do I need to know this? If you were (Name) would you want us discussing this? After creating a good list of responses, have volunteers role-play and practice their skill.

4. **Make a distinction between rumors, griping and gossip.** Bloomfield offers this exercise: First give the definitions, then place rumors, griping and gossip examples on index cards. Place the cards in a container and let each participant choose a card. Divide into small groups and have each group decide: 1) Is the statement rumor, gripe or gossip? 2) If you were the subject of the statement, would you want this being discussed? 3) What are the possible intents of the person who shared this information? and 4)

How would you recommend someone deal with this?

5. **Consider why someone is gossiping and learn from it.** Are volunteers bored and filling up their time with gossip? Are they gossiping as a way to establish friendship? When you understand why someone is a gossiper, then you have valuable information on how to better change their behavior.

6. **Call in expert help when necessary.** If gossip has become gospel, you may want to ask for assistance.

7. **Change gossip content.** Consider encouraging "gossip for good" — focusing on others' successes and good news.

Source: Beth Bloomfield, Director, Retired and Senior Volunteer Program, Volunteer Center Orange County, Santa Ana, CA. Phone (714) 953-5757, ext. 115.

Rumors, Griping and Gossip

What is the distinction among rumors, griping and gossip? Bloomfield says each has a different definition and resolution.

- **Rumors** are about imminent organizational or team issues, such as pending reorganization, staff departures or funding challenges. "The best way to deal with rumors is to keep your volunteers informed about issues that affect them," she says.

- **Griping** is a response to some concrete issue that irritates a volunteer. "The best way to deal with griping is to listen and explore options to remove any real obstacles that are getting between your volunteers and their goals."

- **Gossip** always deals with a topic that doesn't directly affect the people doing the gossiping. It's either about what they heard someone say to somebody else, or even worse, it's about personal affairs of other volunteers or staff members. "The only way to deal with gossip is to check it the moment it comes to your attention and encourage and train the organization's volunteers and staff to do the same," says Bloomfield.

Practice the Four-way Test

When confronted by gossip, volunteers should practice the Four-way Test.

The test involves volunteers asking themselves four questions before they speak:

1. Is it the truth?
2. Is it fair to all concerned?
3. Will it build goodwill and better friendship?
4. Will it be beneficial to all concerned?

"If anyone in our presence engages in gossip that does not pass the Four-way Test, we will gently and firmly address the gossiper at that moment," says Bloomfield.

Youth Volunteers: How to Recruit, Train, Motivate and Reward Young Volunteers.
Edited by Scott C. Stevenson.
© 2010 Stevenson, Inc. Published 2010 by Stevenson, Inc.

Youth Volunteers: How to Recruit, Train, Motivate and Reward Young Volunteers

REACHING OUT TO COLLEGE-AGED VOLUNTEERS

College-aged volunteers can serve as a great volunteer resource providing you can reach them and involve them in some capacity. This age group is sometimes more committed to their volunteer experience because it offers tangible rewards: including the experiences on their resume, allowing them to get a taste of potential career paths and more. Your ability to attract college-aged students will be impacted, in part, by the level of support provided by those colleges and universities with whom you are working.

How to Create Successful College Partnerships

Colleges and universities have a lot of resources, including potential volunteers, and that can make partnerships a success. But those vast resources can also make colleges intimidating.

Jack Foley, vice president for government and community affairs and campus services, Clark University (Worcester, MA), is in charge of an extremely successful partnership between Clark and the Main South Community Development Corp. Together they have been renovating and rebuilding neighborhoods for 20 years. They also won the Carter Partnership Award in 2004.

He says look for these things in a college or university to make a partnership work:

1. **Enlightened self interest.** What are the shared objectives? Foley says right from the beginning their two organizations set out a strategic plan outlining their common goals and how each organization could accomplish them. He advises to not let yourself get sucked into a quick success, make sure your goals are long term and count small successes along the way.

2. **Commitment by the president.** Foley says the college needs to have the backing of the president to make the partnership work. Clark's president set the tone for a successful partnership right from the beginning by building a sense of trust with the neighborhood. He

initiated surveys of the neighbors to address any of their concerns and started to rectify those concerns right away.

3. **Commitment of resources.** A college needs to commit their resources, but not control the entire partnership; the allocation of funds should be a group decision. For example, Clark has one of 15 seats on the Main South CDC's board. While they're involved, they don't control it. "Everyone is making decisions and holding each other accountable," says Foley.

For the last 20 years Clark and Main South CDC have created three strategic plans and have gotten many community organizations involved in their partnership. A bottom-up approach, which includes time, patience and long-term goals has made their partnership a success. He says there are two things to look for in a successful partnership:

1. **What language is used?** Does the "we" include the partnership or the college? Is it your agenda or the institution's agenda?

2. **Who controls the money?** If both partners don't decide how funds are spent, they aren't on equal footing.

Source: Jack Foley, Vice President for Government and Community Affairs, Clark University, Worcester, MA. Phone (508) 793-7444. E-mail: jfoley@clarku.edu

Are Your Community's Schools Including Service in Curriculum?

Today, most colleges and universities include questions about volunteerism or community service on application forms. Many cite the importance for students to be familiar with the needs of the community at large and with ways to contribute to the common good.

As a result, nonprofit organizations of all types are more compelled to develop or expand volunteer opportunities that appeal to adolescents and encourage them to continue as active volunteers after high school.

Some of the nation's largest schools have even implemented community service as a graduation

requirement.

The ways students can fulfill requirements are as varied as are the types of service, and most school districts allowing a significant amount of latitude in qualifying projects.

Many charities have found ways to allow young people who volunteer to meet the requirements and have generally been pleased with the results. Students often bring the enthusiasm of youth along with skills that adults don't always have, including computer knowledge.

REACHING OUT TO COLLEGE-AGED VOLUNTEERS

College Students Help to Increase Volunteer Base

The International Institute of Metropolitan St. Louis (St. Louis, MO) turns to college students to maintain and enhance its volunteer base.

"Young adults are a wonderful resource," says Sarah Bekemeyer, community outreach specialist. "They are inquisitive and eager to learn and develop new skills, friends and knowledge base. Many have a school requirement to fulfill public service hours and others just want to make a difference."

Bekemeyer and her co-workers reach out to college students at activity fairs and by contacting student organizations.

To recruit volunteers from this crowd, Bekemeyer says:

- **Visit local college and university websites** or contact their student life/activities centers for lists of student clubs and organizations. Next, send the leader of each group an e-mail with information about your volunteer opportunities, asking that the information be shared with the group's members.

- **Attend college activity fairs,** being sure to display information on current opportunities, volunteer applications and general information about your nonprofit. Include a display board with pictures of your nonprofit and volunteers in action, and offer inexpensive giveaways like pens, pins or bookmarks. To get people to your booth, start the conversation. Don't just sit there and wait for people to come to you. Stand in front of your booth, greet people and ask what volunteer activities interest them. Tell them what opportunities you have that match their interests and have a sign-up sheet ready so you can follow up with them later.

To ensure young adults take the commitment of volunteering seriously, Bekemeyer says, ask if their schedule permits a commitment, stress the importance of contacting you if they cannot make their scheduled volunteer activity and treat volunteerism as if it were a job or class.

Source: Sarah Bekemeyer, Community Outreach Specialist, International Institute of Metropolitan St. Louis, St. Louis, MO. Phone (314) 773-9090. E-mail: bekemeyers@iistl.org

Online Site Helps Connect With College Volunteers

Looking for a go-to spot on college and university campuses to recruit volunteers?

Karen Partridge, communications manager, Campus Compact (Providence, RI), says they partner with more than 1,000 colleges and universities to help establish relations with community organizations across the country.

"Campus Compact helps build strong campus-community ties while providing volunteer managers a resource to recruit volunteers on campus," says Partridge.

Volunteer managers can utilize www.compact.org, to access the following resources:

- **Program models.** Visitors can access more than 700 established program models used by colleges and universities to create relationships with their community.

- **Promise of Partnerships.** Partridge says the Promise of Partnerships is a volunteer manager's guide to tapping into local colleges and universities' resources. The publication offers advice on making the right contacts, planning effective partnerships and working with students and faculty. The book also features tips, checklists and best practices.

- **Online volunteer opportunities list.** Community-based organizations can post their volunteer opportunities at: www.compact.org/opportunities/volunteer. Some 9,800 college students, faculty and campus community service directors visit the site weekly.

- **Search by state to locate colleges/universities.** The site offers volunteer managers the option to select the state in which they are interested and view their members.

Source: Karen Partridge, Communications Manager, Campus Compact, Brown University, Providence, RI. Phone (401) 867-3922. E-mail: kpartridge@compact.org

REACHING OUT TO COLLEGE-AGED VOLUNTEERS

Learn From a Volunteer Program That Has Its 'ACT' Together

Thirty percent of the 2,000 students who attend Carleton College (Northfield, MN) are active volunteers, logging nearly 4,000 combined hours of volunteer work each term.

Although Carleton certainly fosters a volunteer-oriented environment on campus with the help of the Acting in the Community Together (ACT) program, about 80 percent of incoming freshmen have already had a long career of volunteerism according to ACT Director Laura Riehle-Merrill.

Begun in 1985, this student-run program is one of the longest standing of its kind in the state of Minnesota. Carleton students venture into the community and surrounding areas to volunteer with community partner organizations including Habitat for Humanity, Adopt-a-Highway, Red Cross, Northfield's Community Action Center and the Northfield Hospital. ACT participants will also answer a call for tutoring in the local community when the need arises.

"Our community partners are amazing," Riehle-Merrill said. "They're acting as co-educators of our students by nurturing them and helping them understand their contributions are important."

With 41 ongoing volunteer programs, the ACT program requires dedicated staffers to allow the program to run smoothly. In addition to three full-time professional staff, each ACT program has a team of two to four volunteer student leaders or program directors. Additionally, the program hosts a team of 10 paid student coordinators who work in the center supervising and supporting the more than 80 volunteer program directors.

This call to activism seems to carry on throughout a Carleton graduate's lifetime. The school has one of the highest numbers of former students engaged in the Peace Corps and Teach for America. Further proof is that nearly 89 percent of former student coordinators and 92 percent of program directors of the ACT program say that participation in the program engaged these individuals to a lifetime of involvement.

How can the success of ACT energize your student population and community?

- **Give lots of choices.** The program offers a wide array of volunteer opportunities along with a number of commitment levels. Students can fit hours of volunteer time into their weekly schedule or partake in the one-time volunteer opportunities available each term.

- **Use positive peer pressure.** Peer influence is one way this program has energized the student workers. Much of the success of the program is attributed to positive word-of-mouth buzz from student to student.

- **Student input and opportunities.** Carleton students see a program run by students for students with leadership opportunities. Riehle-Merrill said the programs encompassed within ACT fill a community need and fuel student passion.

- **Building community partnerships** with area nonprofits that foster student education and that value students as an asset to the community.

- **Communication is key.** Community partnerships with nonprofits help educate students as to why their role is important. A small task such as assisting a nonprofit stuff envelopes can be more meaningful if the student is educated on the result of the mail campaign.

- **Leadership opportunities.** The ACT program offers leadership roles such as student coordinators and program directors.

- **Recognition.** ACT hosts an annual banquet to bring the student volunteers and community partnership nonprofits to one table for a night of thanks and gratitude.

Source: Laura Riehle-Merrill, Carleton ACT Director, Carleton College, Northfield, MN. Phone (507) 222-7020. E-mail: lriehlem@carleton.edu

Campus Compact Involves Students Community Service

More and more colleges and universities across the nation are becoming involved in community service. Many of those institutions are looking for projects to interest their students, faculty and staff.

Campus Compact is a national coalition of more than 1,100 college and university presidents committed to the civic purposes of higher education. To support this civic mission, Campus Compact promotes community service that develops students' citizenship skills and values, encourages partnership between campuses and communities and assists faculty who seek to integrate public and community

engagement into their teaching and research.

CampusCares is a partner in Campus Compact and is an organization devoted to providing information about member college campuses around the country. The CampusCares website provides an overview of community service and civic engagement — what the terms mean, what those on campus are doing, and where to go for more information. Plus, you'll find ideas and examples useful to those interested in increasing their campus service activities.

For more info: Campus Compact, www.compact.org; CampusCares, www.campuscares.org

REACHING OUT TO COLLEGE-AGED VOLUNTEERS

Recruit Male Volunteers Through Fraternities

Campus fraternities are a great resource for recruiting male volunteers, specifically for fundraising events and one-time projects.

For several years, Jason Hecker, executive director, Literacy Center West (Cincinnati, OH), has partnered with a local fraternity, Beta Theta Pi at the University of Cincinnati. The fraternity plans and manages the Psychedelic Toilet Seat Sale, which raises $3,000 annually for the organization. Hecker says while in college he was a member of the

---

Tips for Building Fraternity Relationships

Like both Literacy Center West (Cincinnati, OH) and Little Brothers — Friends of the Elderly (Hancock, MI), once the initial fraternity connections are made, the beneficial relationship can continue for years. The fraternity can end up adopting your cause and coming back year after year with new members.

To get a good start at building a relationship, Hecker advises attending your local campus' Fraternity Council's meetings. The meetings, which are open to the public, allow the council to get to know your face, who you are and your cause.

You can also contact individual houses and ask for the name, number and e-mail of the philanthropy chair to schedule a face-to-face meeting.

---

same fraternity and approached them about organizing a fundraising event for Literacy Center West. He says the fraternity wanted to take full credit for raising the funds and came up with the idea of a toilet seat sale — people pay to drop painted toilet seats in the yards of friends and neighbors, who in turn pay to have them removed.

Hecker says from the partnership some fraternity members have grown to become regular volunteers, board members and staff.

Cathy Aten, volunteer program coordinator, Little Brothers — Friends of the Elderly, Upper Michigan Chapter (Hancock, MI), says since 1982, 10 to 12 fraternities have volunteered to help with the organization's wood-cutting program with about half of them doing it on a regular basis. Aten says from September to November fraternities on weekends cut, split, stack and deliver wood to clients, who use the wood to heat their homes all winter. Aten says the unique, physical project is perfect for fraternity members — young, strong men — who may never have had a similar experience.

Sources: Jason Hecker, Executive Director, Literacy Center West, Cincinnati, OH. Phone (513) 244-5062.
E-mail: Jason@litcenterwest.org
Cathy Aten, Volunteer Program Coordinator, Little Brothers — Friends of the Elderly, Upper Michigan Chapter, Hancock, MI. Phone (906) 482-6944. E-mail: caten.hou@littlebrothers.org

Tips on Partnering With Colleges for Internship Programs

Partnerships with colleges and universities can produce a highly effective internship program.

Allison Oja, senior specialist for volunteer services — clinics and interns, Park Nicollet Health Services (St. Louis Park, MN), runs a successful non-clinical internships program. The program places college and high school students in noninvasive healthcare opportunities, including: medical receptionists, music therapy and physical therapy.

Oja has formed partnerships with seven local colleges and universities over the past four years. She offers these tips when forming partnerships:

- Both sides must be clear about expectations from the outset. Communicate in person how your program works and ask what the school hopes to achieve.

- Bring materials illustrating how the program works, including: induction checklists, orientation manuals, application packets and job descriptions.

- Appoint a single person liaison to the school. Talking to one person makes it easier to check on student progress.

Source: Allison Oja, Senior Specialist, Volunteer Services — Clinics and Interns, Park Nicollet Health Services, St. Louis Park, MN. Phone (952) 993-1786. E-mail: ojaae@parknicollet.com

Youth Volunteers: How to Recruit, Train, Motivate and Reward Young Volunteers

ALL ABOUT INTERNSHIPS

Internships can be a win-win for everyone involved as long as the program has the level of internal attention and support that it deserves. Often a well-prepared intern can provide your office with services and project responsibilities that might not otherwise be possible. In addition to adequate planning, the selection procedures you follow are key to placing top interns with your organization.

What You Need to Know to Start an Intern Program

Interns can make a big impact in your organization. When you have extra work or something with a deadline, with little or no money, interns can be a big help.

Larissa Bailiff coordinates the Museum of Modern Art's (New York, NY) decade-old formal internship program, which includes 100 interns. Here are things she says to consider before hiring an intern:

1. **Devote time to interns.** Don't expect interns to jump in and take loads off your hands. You need to be able to delegate and explain tasks — if you don't, interns can get frustrated and mistakes can be made, taking up more of your time.

2. **Treat interns like staff members.** Provide them a table or desk, computer and phone — all necessary tools to get the job done. Introduce them to their supervisor and make sure they know to whom to report.

3. **Set clear expectations.** Many interns fill school requirements and their internship positions must fit into a time frame. It's also good to set time limits on positions and to make sure your intern is committed to that time frame.

4. **Be prepared to write letters of recommendation.** Many interns look at an internship as an opportunity to build their resumes. Bailiff says a large part of the museum's staff is made of former interns.

5. **Request letters of recommendation**. Make sure the intern is personable and independent, can travel and handle responsibility and will complete the position's duration. A great way to get this information is by asking for letters of recommendation from professional references. Bailiff warns against prima donnas, or people who think they are above the position.

Source: Larissa Bailiff, Internship Coordinator, The Museum of Modern Art, New York, NY. Phone (212) 408-8440. E-mail: Larissa_bailiff@moma.org

Consider the Benefits of Internships

Has your organization ever created one or more internship positions? Internships can benefit virtually any type of organization. They can be structured for a brief period (i.e., one month) or for longer periods (i.e., six months or a year). They can be paid or unpaid positions.

Although internships are generally geared toward college/university students, it's also possible to tailor them toward high school students.

Why consider internships? Here are some benefits for both the sponsoring organization and the intern:

Benefits to the organization:

- Service from an intern for a specified period of time.
- Concentrated efforts on a particular project —

conducting a survey, writing feature stories, developing an orientation manual, etc.

- Gaining positive public recognition as a good corporate citizen — helping a local student learn more about public service, helping him/her with career preparation.

Benefits to the intern:

- Hands-on experience in career preparation.
- An accomplishment to list on his/her pre-graduation resume.
- An opportunity to test the waters with a particular job experience.
- Sometimes, the opportunity to get paid for real work.

ALL ABOUT INTERNSHIPS

Eight Steps to Build or Revive an Intern Program

Whether you want to build a volunteer intern program from scratch or revive a failing one, there are steps you can take to get your program on the right track.

Since 1975, officials with the Minneapolis Institute of Arts' Education Division (Minneapolis, MN) have coordinated a museum-wide internship program. About 25 volunteer interns work with the museum annually exploring their chosen professional field.

Treden Wagoner, coordinator of the intern program for the last 12 years, says while there are handbooks offering advice for building an intern program, the best way to get started is networking with similar organizations that have an established program.

"You can learn a lot from colleagues about what to do and what not to do," says Wagoner.

He offers this outline to build or revive an intern program:

1. **Identify your organization's goals.**

2. **Develop a recruitment strategy.** Will you recruit for specific positions or accept general applications? From where will the candidates come? How will prospective interns find out about the program?

3. **Identify existing resources that can be utilized (e.g., college career centers and career websites).**

4. **Establish an application procedure.** What information do you need from candidates? How will you collect it? How often will you recruit? "Handbooks and samples from other organizations can provide a basis for how to create an application form and give an idea of what information is important to collect," he says.

5. **Design the placement process.** How will you decide who gets the internship? Is there a placement committee? Is it the coordinator's job?

6. **Form a standard intern orientation.** Include policies and procedures that apply to volunteers, such as those for safety and emergencies.

7. **Create intern and program evaluations.** Wagoner says an evaluation plan can be designed starting with your program goals and outcomes. Ask yourself, "Are our interns meeting our organization's goals? How do we measure success?"

8. **Determine a tracking system for statistics (e.g., how many interns, how many hours, which projects, etc.)** Statistics are a way to measure success and provide a quantitative way to discuss the program.

Source: Treden Wagoner, Coordinator of Education Technology Programs, The Minneapolis Institute of Arts, Minneapolis, MN. Phone (612) 870-3189. E-mail: twagoner@artsmia.org

Ensure Your Program's Success

Treden Wagoner, coordinator of education technology programs, the Minneapolis Institute of Arts (Minneapolis, MN), says once an intern program is established, implementing the following elements will ensure its success:

- Appoint a go-to person. Wagoner says there needs to be an individual whose responsibility it is to coordinate the program for the entire organization. "This is an excellent opportunity for centralization. It is more difficult to maintain those things that make a program successful for the organization and for the interns when individuals recruit their own interns."

- Develop a clear means of communication. Communication between candidates and the organization begins with promotional materials (e.g., flyers, Web postings, e-mails, etc.). Candidates should know who to contact with questions.

- Create staff buy-in. Wagoner says if staff members don't understand the value of working with interns, they won't participate in the program, creating one more obstacle to obtaining success.

- Establish clear goals. Developing intern projects and job descriptions with intern supervisors is one way an intern coordinator can contribute to the program's success, Wagoner says.

ALL ABOUT INTERNSHIPS

Make Your Intern's Experience Rewarding

Internships, if prepared and carried out properly, can provide a mutually beneficial experience for both the organization and the intern.

To be sure the experience is most productive, follow these steps:

1. **Provide a clear picture.** Be sure both you and the potential intern know his/her anticipated duties before agreeing to the arrangement. Make intern qualifications well known in advance, and share a job description during the interview process.

2. **Limit the scope of the intern's duties.** While some variety is advised, responsibilities should remain focused so the individual can experience accomplishment throughout the duration of the position and develop an understanding for certain aspects of your organization.

3. **Treat interns as you would staff. Include them in meetings.** Expect them to show up for work on time. You are preparing them for the real world and would do them a disservice if your expectations were any less.

4. **Challenge them.** Ask your intern to share a report at a board or volunteer meeting. Call on him/her during staff meetings. Risk-taking should be a part of the learning experience.

5. **Ask for weekly management reports.** Have the intern complete a weekly report listing the previous week's accomplishments, lists appointments for the current week and prioritizes projects and tasks. The form will help keep the intern more accountable to both you and him/herself.

6. **Nurture their experience.** In addition to having the intern sit in on staff meetings, meet regularly with him/her to go over projects, answer questions and offer support.

It's not uncommon to have interns who eventually return as full-time employees. If you think of each intern in that light, you will more likely provide him/her with the attention and experience he/she deserves.

Internships Give Volunteers Professional Career Options

Offer value-added opportunities such as internships as incentive for current volunteers to sign on for additional hours and newcomers to sign up to help your cause.

The Gaston Hospice and Grief Counseling Services (Gastonia, NC) partners with area nursing schools, universities and the local high school to offer internships to students interested in the fields of nursing, counseling and social work.

Interns take part in hands-on work with patients and gain significant career experience. For example, social work and counseling interns manage a caseload just like paid social workers or counselors, gaining a realistic idea of the profession's day-to-day obligations. These interns are supervised by the social work manager and director of counseling services. Counseling interns also work with community grief clients as well as hospice families.

Because of the internship program, Gaston Hospice has four nursing school student interns and four counseling and social work interns at any given time.

Jennifer Jones, volunteer coordinator, offers suggestions to provide successful internship opportunities for area students:

❑ First and foremost, be sure the clinical staff is on board with the partnership program and agreeable to working with interns. Gaston Hospice clinical staff recognize the inherent value of their interns and appreciate the additional assistance for the patients' well-being.

❑ Limit intern opportunities to a comfortable level where staff can handle additional efforts needed to manage intern staff and are also able to provide the appropriate environment for the interns to learn.

❑ Offer career opportunities to interns completing their coursework within your institution. Encourage interns who have worked within your organization to apply for long-term career positions. At Gaston Hospice, employment opportunities are listed at the hospital system's website and staff work with interns to offer them career placement within the organization.

Source: Jennifer Jones, Volunteer Coordinator, Gaston Hospice and Grief Counseling Services, Gastonia, NC. Phone (704) 861-8405. E-mail: cunningj@gmh.org

ALL ABOUT INTERNSHIPS

Organized Objectives Help Staff Buy in to Intern Program

One of the biggest concerns when creating an internship program is whether your staff will buy in to the project.

That concern is warranted, since your organization's staff will be the ones working directly with the interns, taking the time to teach them and allowing them to job shadow.

When Denise Lamphier, director, volunteer services, La Porte Regional Health System (La Porte, IN), created her VolunTeen student internship program (see brochure, below), she wanted to make sure the students, age 14 to 18, got an opportunity for a hands-on learning experience.

Twenty-seven hospital departments — from family practice to the cancer center to medical records — take part in the VolunTeen program. Throughout the school year, and during a special summer session, these departments allow a student to volunteer for four hours a week and see first-hand what they do.

To get staff from these departments to buy in to the project, Lamphier worked with one of the hospital's clinical educators to develop student objective sheets. Lamphier then worked with each department director to adjust objective sheets to specific departments.

With this tool in hand, she says, department staff knew how they were expected to interact with the students, and the students knew what to expect as well.

Lamphier says the student objective sheets come in especially handy when a new staff person comes on who hasn't worked with the interns yet. The staff person can look at the objective sheet and know exactly what the intern can do or needs to do. She says both the staff and department directors feel more comfortable with the process.

Source: Denise Lamphier, Director Volunteer Services, La Porte Regional Health System, La Porte, IN. Phone (219) 325-5418. E-mail: d.lamphier@lph.org

Start at the Top for Staff Buy-in

Why don't staff buy in to the value of volunteers?

Perhaps they don't know volunteers' relevance to the organization. Maybe they're unsure what to do with volunteers or feel they infringe on staff duties. Whatever the reason, lack of buy-in of volunteers' value can lead to an underused program and poor volunteer retention rates.

Jennifer Gilligan Cole, president, Cole Community Concepts (Nashville, TN), says she has seen many volunteer managers try to fix volunteer/staff relations on a small level when the solution lies with an organization's top management.

To create staff buy-in, Cole says, ask your CEO and board to define volunteering. Approach upper management by showing them how volunteers fit into and enhance a successful business strategy.

First, show these key players how volunteers make a positive financial impact on the organization (e.g., what would happen to the organization if there were no volunteers?).

Secondly, consider the amount of staff time it actually takes to manage volunteers. Cole says she recently told a nonprofit's board its staff spends 30 percent of their time managing volunteers. The board had no idea.

Upper management needs to recognize the amount of time staff manages volunteers by giving them performance reviews and support, she says. Once you emphasize to upper management just how critical volunteers are to fulfilling the mission of the organization, their buy-in will help get other staff to value and support volunteer involvement.

Maintaining communication between staff and volunteers is crucial. Cole says that apart from orientation, many organizations never revisit the roles for staff and volunteers. She suggests holding quarterly or bi-annual check-in sessions for both staff and volunteers. These meetings provide an opportunity to address concerns about roles and responsibilities before they rise to the level of conflicts.

The sessions will empower staff and volunteers, Cole says, while raising retention rates.

Source: Jennifer Gilligan Cole, President, Cole Community Concepts, Nashville, TN. Phone (615) 969-6424. E-mail: colecommunity@comcast.net

Content not available in this edition

Youth Volunteers: How to Recruit, Train, Motivate and Reward Young Volunteers

IDEAS FOR RECOGNIZING YOUTH'S CONTRIBUTIONS

How are you recognizing your young volunteers? Are the methods you use different than the ways in which you applaud adult volunteers? Do you show appreciation daily in small ways in addition to more significant ways at various times throughout the year? This chapter offers ideas on how you can recognize and reward younger volunteers in ways that are most meaningful to them.

Five Ways to Recognize High School Volunteers

If you rely on high-school-aged volunteers, you know that the ways used to recognize and affirm them are different from methods you may use with other volunteers. They're a special group that requires special types of recognition.

Use any of these methods to pat your high school volunteers on the back:

1. Find out when all-school assemblies are scheduled and get permission to make a special award just prior to the main event — while you have a captive audience.

2. Do a brief kudos article for the school newspaper or newsletter that praises your high school volunteers. Your students will love being recognized among their peers.

3. Write an unsolicited letter of reference — To Whom It May Concern — delineating a student volunteer's accomplishments. Give it to the student to use for landing a summer job or to include with college entrance materials.

4. Write a letter of commendation to the parents of the student volunteer praising his/her values and work ethic. What better reward could a parent ask for than to have a child praised for a job well done? Chances are the student won't mind hearing about the letter as well.

5. Identify various student awards/recognition given throughout your community — mayor's youth commission, student of the month, etc. — and nominate your top student volunteers for the honor.

Do Something Awards: The Oscars of Youth Volunteering

Now's the time to honor your favorite youth volunteer for a national Do Something Award. Honoring community and philanthropic activism, the awards are given yearly during a nationally televised broadcast on a major network.

Katherine Cheng, associate with the Do Something organization (New York, NY), says the awards are the equivalent to the Oscars for youth volunteering.

The awards, originally named the BR!CK awards when started in 1996, are open to anyone 25 and younger in the United States or Canada. An application can be submitted directly from Do Something's website, www.dosomething.org.

Cheng says five winners, selected by a committee of past winners and experts, will each receive $10,000 in scholarship and community grants, paid directly to their nonprofit of choice. The winners may also choose to receive $5,000 of the total money awarded in an educational scholarship. The grand prize winner will receive $100,000.

The committee members look for the best-of-the-class volunteer projects that cover a diversity of issues, interests and talents, she says. Past winners include volunteers who have formed their own nonprofits to start youth programs, raise funds for the homeless, and economically and socially rebuild communities overseas.

For the 2010 awards, applications must be submitted by March 1, 2010. Each applicant must include a letter of recommendation. Cheng says the letters should illuminate the work and impact of the volunteer's project and the writer should be a non-family member who can speak in detail about the volunteer's work.

In addition to the Do Something awards, Cheng says they give out one $500 grant weekly to volunteers who send in project ideas and need funding to get them off the ground.

Considered the Oscars of youth volunteering, Do Something awards honor persons 25 or younger. Application deadline is March 1, 2010. Log on to www.dosomething.org

Source: Katherine Cheng, Associate, Do Something Awards, Do Something, New York, NY. Phone (212) 254-2390, ext. 223. E-mail: kcheng@dosomething.org

Youth Volunteers: How to Recruit, Train, Motivate and Reward Young Volunteers

IDEAS FOR RECOGNIZING YOUTH'S CONTRIBUTIONS

Honor Youth Volunteers for Outstanding Acts of Volunteerism

The Prudential Spirit of Community Awards committee will begin taking applications for the 2011 awards starting in August. Applicants for the 2010 awards program honoring youth volunteers deadline was Oct. 31, 2009.

All public and private middle and high schools in the United States, as well as all Girl Scout councils, 4-H organizations, American Red Cross chapters, YMCAs and volunteer centers are eligible to select a student nominee. Here's how the process works:

✓ **Local honorees:** Nearly 4,500 local honorees are reviewed by state-level judges. Judges name two honorees from each state and the District of Columbia based on criteria such as personal initiative, creativity, effort, impact and personal growth. State honorees are announced each February.

✓ **State honorees:** State honorees receive $1,000, an engraved silver medallion, all-expense-paid trip in early May to Washington, DC, for several days of national recognition events.

✓ **National honorees:** Finally, five middle level and five high school students are named national honorees by a prestigious national selection committee in May. These honorees receive additional $5,000 awards, gold medallions, crystal trophies and $5,000 grants from The Prudential Foundation for nonprofit, charitable organizations of their choice.

The organization receives nearly 20,000 entries each year for the nation-wide program honoring young people for outstanding acts of volunteerism conducted by Prudential Financial, Inc. (Newark, NJ) in partnership with the National Association of Secondary School Principals (Reston, VA). To submit an entry, go to www.prudential.com/spirit.

About the Awards Program...

Now in its 15th year, the Prudential Spirit of Community Awards program is the United States' largest youth recognition program based exclusively on volunteer community service. The program was created in 1995 by Prudential (Newark, NJ) in partnership with the National Association of Secondary School Principals (Reston, VA) to honor middle and high school students for outstanding service to others at the local, state and national level.

The program's goals are to applaud young people already making a positive difference in their towns and neighborhoods, and to inspire others to think about how they might contribute to their communities. Over the past 14 years, more than 260,000 young Americans have participated in the program, and nearly 90,000 of them have been officially recognized for their volunteer work.

The Prudential Spirit of Community Awards program is also conducted in Japan, South Korea, Taiwan and Ireland.

Scholarship Program Celebrates Young Volunteers

On June 25, 2009, as part of the Kohl's Kids Who Care® Scholarship Program, Kohl's Department Stores (Menomonee Falls, WI) honored more than 2,000 young people nationwide for good deeds they performed in their communities through volunteerism.

These winners have qualified for the chance to receive a $1,000 regional scholarship for post-secondary education. Of the regional winners, Kohl's will then award 10 national winners an additional $5,000 scholarship for their outstanding service and donate $1,000 to a nonprofit organization of each of the national winners' choice.

Since its inception in 2001, the Kohl's Kids Who Care Scholarship Program has given more than $1.8 million in scholarships and prizes to recognize and reward young volunteers.

"We are proud to recognize so many young kids who are volunteering to help benefit their communities," says Julie Gardner, executive vice president and chief marketing officer at Kohl's. "The Kohl's Kids Who Care Scholarship Program allows us to reward kids who are doing selfless acts across the country." Learn more at: www.kohlscorporation.com/communityrelations/scholarship/index.asp

Become a Sleuth for Recognition Clues

All volunteers should be thanked often — but what to give or what to do? In your everyday conversations with volunteers, listen for clues that may spark a creative recognition idea. For example, what are the topics that really pique their interest? Do they light up when you ask about their friends? Do they always have a story to tell you about their pets? Do they have a sport or local sports team about which they are

particularly passionate? Are they active in their church or synagogue?

Recognition is more meaningful if it is personalized. Any gift that says, "I listened when you told me about yourself" tells every volunteer what they need to know — that they are valuable — to you and to your organization.

47

IDEAS FOR RECOGNIZING YOUTH'S CONTRIBUTIONS

Daily Point of Light Award Honors Volunteers

Are you looking for a way to recognize someone whose volunteering efforts are extraordinary? Why not nominate him or her for a Daily Point of Light Award.

The Daily Point of light award, established in 1989, honors persons and volunteer groups who have made a commitment to their communities by meeting critical needs found in their communities. One award is given each weekday.

The Daily Point of Light Awards are given to individuals who find innovative ways to meet needs found in their communities. The effort they make often leads to long-term solutions for outstanding community problems. The following criteria, taken from the Points of Light Website (www.pointsoflight.org/recognition/dpol), are utilized in reviewing and judging nominations:

- **Community needs and solutions** — Activity must meet a community need or concern and serve those who are disconnected from the larger community. Is there a long-term solution, or does the effort give the recipient the tools they need to achieve a solution on their own?
- **Connections building** — Hands-on service that results in building connections between the community and those who may be isolated from it.
- **Ongoing involvement** — To be eligible, an activity should be at least six months in duration. One exception is the category of disaster relief. Nominations that do not meet these criteria can be held for later consideration.
- **Impact** — Demonstrated real impact from the activity.
- **Innovation** — Activity should reflect innovative or unique approaches to solving serious social problems.

Any individual, organization, group, family or business actively involved in a voluntary service directed at domestic or international problem-solving may apply for a Daily Point of Light Award.

For more information go to: www.dailypointoflight.org

Teen Earns Award for Extraordinary Volunteering Efforts

Teens throughout the country are lending a hand to causes they care deeply about — and, in the case of Dallas Jessup (Vancouver, WA), starting nonprofits to help achieve their goals.

At age 14, Jessup created the nonprofit, Just Yell Fire (Vancouver, WA). She gathered community support to make an instructional video illustrating ways teen girls can fight back from attempted sexual assault or abduction, tapping her skills as a black belt and a trained Filipino street fighter.

Now a high school senior, Jessup has logged more than 3,000 volunteer hours managing the nonprofit. She has traveled innumerable miles — averag-

Content not available in this edition

Dallas Jessup

ing 10,000 miles a month — across the country to conduct presentations about her life-saving techniques.

Jessup also created a DVD of her techniques, distributing 680,000 copies and reaching millions of girls in 42 countries. In summer 2008, she toured India to speak to thousands of high school and university students.

Her safety film is used by police agencies, schools, shelters, teachers and parents.

"Millions of girls are now fighting back against abduction and sexual assault because of our Just Yell Fire nonprofit," Jessup says. "We are proud of these results from our all-volunteer organization protecting the most vulnerable members of society — girls age 11 to 19."

For her extraordinary efforts, Jessup earned a Daily Points of Light Award from the Points of Light Institute. Learn more about her efforts at www.justyellfire.com.

Source: Dallas Jessup, Founder and Spokesperson, Just Yell Fire, Vancouver, WA. Phone (360) 521-0437. E-mail: info@justyellfire.com

Honor Dedicated Volunteers with Unique, Inspiring Gift

Looking for a gift idea for dedicated volunteers? Consider giving them a copy of "Chicken Soup for the Volunteer's Soul: 101 Stories to Celebrate the Spirit of Caring, Courage, and Compassion" by Jack Canfield.

The book is filled with inspiring stories from such leading volunteer organizations as the American Red Cross, Big Brothers Big Sisters, Habitat for Humanity, Muscular Dystrophy Association, Peace Corps, Rotary International, Special Olympics and The Salvation Army.

A portion of the proceeds from the sale of the book is donated to the Points of Light Foundation and Volunteer Center National Network.

The book is available online at www.amazon.com or www.bn.com.